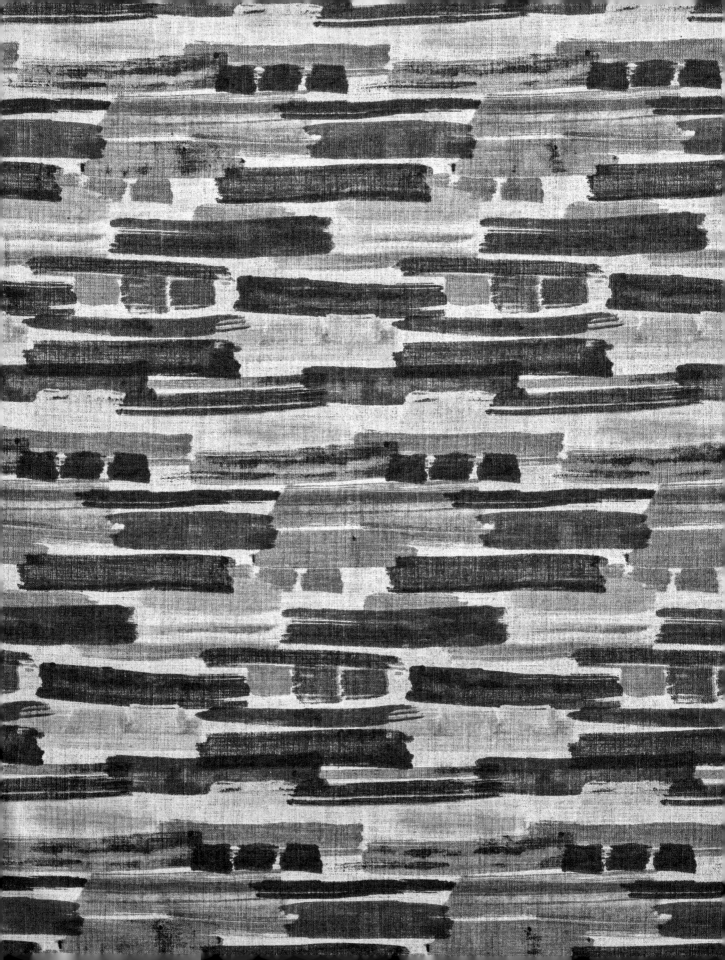

YASSOU

*a Greek term used as a casual greeting or farewell,
to wish another good health, or while raising a glass*

YASSOU

The Simple, Seasonal Mediterranean Cooking of Greece

SHAILY LIPA

ARTISAN
NEW YORK

Library of Congress Cataloging-in-Publication Data

Names: Lipa, Shaily, author.
Title: Yassou : the simple, seasonal Mediterranean cooking of Greece / Shaily Lipa.
Description: New York : Artisan, 2024. | Includes index. |
Identifiers: LCCN 2023050017 | ISBN 9781648291852 (hardback)
Subjects: LCSH: Cooking, Mediterranean. | Cooking, Greek. | LCGFT: Cookbooks.
Classification: LCC TX725.M35 L567 2024 | DDC 641.59/1822—dc23/eng/20231122
LC record available at https://lccn.loc.gov/2023050017

Design by Suet Chong
Food styling by Amit Farber
Cover design by Suet Chong

Artisan books may be purchased in bulk for business, educational, or promotional use. For information, please contact your local bookseller or the Hachette Book Group Special Markets Department at special.markets@hbgusa.com.

The publisher is not responsible for websites (or their content) that are not owned by the publisher.

The Hachette Speakers Bureau provides a wide range of authors for speaking events. To find out more, go to hachettespeakersbureau.com or email HachetteSpeakers@hbgusa.com.

Published by Artisan,
an imprint of Workman Publishing,
a division of Hachette Book Group, Inc.
1290 Avenue of the Americas
New York, NY 10104
artisanbooks.com

The Artisan name and logo are registered trademarks of Hachette Book Group, Inc.

Printed in China on responsibly sourced paper
First printing, April 2024

10 9 8 7 6 5 4 3 2 1

*To my Greek grandparents,
Levana and Angel,
with whom I had many
unforgettable Greek meals*

CONTENTS

Introduction 9

As we journey south, the landscape opens to sun-drenched coastlines and the sparkling expanse of the Mediterranean Sea. The seafood from this region is renowned, one of the great culinary treasures of Greece. Traditional preparations enhance the fresh seafood without overpowering its flavor: Grilled octopus glistens from a marinade of red wine and vinegar (page 62), shrimp are poached and enriched with a mixture of olive oil and lemon (page 67), calamari rings are coated in flour and fried until golden (page 61), and fish is elegantly seasoned with herbs and lemon.

The food you will find in Greece today is not so different from what the Greeks ate hundreds of years ago. But what we view as traditional Greek cuisine is actually a reflection of the country's long history as both conqueror and conquest before the establishment of the First Hellenic Republic, and also a culinary fusion emerging from the crossroads of Europe, Africa, and Asia.

Venetians ruled over parts of Greece from the thirteenth to the eighteenth centuries, particularly the Ionian Islands and Crete. They introduced to Greeks novel ingredients and culinary techniques that seamlessly blended with the native traditions. For example, pasta, a Venetian staple, led to the creation of what is now Pastitsio, a baked pasta dish that has evolved to include layers of ground meat and béchamel sauce (page 214).

Venetian trade routes opened a world of spices to Greece, introducing nutmeg, cinnamon, and cloves, which infused local dishes with new flavors. These warming aromatics are now hallmarks of dishes like Pastitsada, a hearty chicken stew with a scented tomato sauce served over a bed of pasta (page 194). Today, pastitsada is a culinary mainstay, especially on the island of Corfu.

From the fifteenth to the early nineteenth centuries, the Venetians slowly lost their control of the majority of Greek land to the Ottoman Empire. The Ottomans ruled mainland Greece for more than four hundred years, and arguably had the greatest impact on the native cuisine. Among the notable influences were specific cooking techniques such as wrapping and grilling, which gave rise to what are now iconic dishes like stuffed grape leaves, stuffed cabbage, and souvlaki (grilled skewered meat). Rice and pastries, staple ingredients in many Greek dishes, are also considered contributions from the Ottoman world.

This confluence of culinary influences has given rise to what we know today as the Mediterranean diet.

The Secrets of the Mediterranean Diet

The phenomenon of the Mediterranean diet first entered the zeitgeist in the 1950s. Research known as the Seven Countries Study surveyed the dietary habits of the people of Greece, Italy, Yugoslavia (modern-day Serbia and Croatia), Japan, Finland, the Netherlands, and the United States. One of the most important findings was that Mediterranean populations, compared to Northern Europeans and Americans, enjoyed overall higher life expectancies with lower rates of chronic diseases. The Greek island of Crete stood out as a beacon of exceptional health and longevity. The study attributed these longer and healthier life spans to the regular consumption of olive oil, grains, fruits, and wild and cultivated greens; moderate intake of wine; and limited amounts of red meat.

Many other studies have since confirmed the findings of the Seven Countries Study. The Blue Zones study, an ongoing research project that explores factors that contribute to longevity in regions known as Blue Zones, has found that the island of Ikaria has some of the highest rates of centenarians (those who live to be 100 years of age or more) and some of the lowest rates of dementia, heart disease, and other chronic illnesses in the world thanks to their dietary habits, active lifestyles, and close-knit culture.

Greeks are the first to tell you that their cuisine is as good for the body as it is for the spirit. This wisdom was inherited from their ancient ancestors, in fact: even Hippocrates emphasized the importance of a balanced diet to maintaining physical health, which in turn contributed to mental and moral health. Throughout history, while other cultures have industrialized their foods and ways of cooking, Greeks have stayed connected to their local food systems and continue to cook foods that are simple, fresh, and nourishing.

The Mediterranean diet represents more than just a collection of recipes; it embodies an entire philosophy of healthy living that includes nutrition, community, and an active lifestyle. Its enduring popularity and scientific backing only attest to its power in promoting longevity, vitality, and overall well-being.

About This Book

Yassou is your guide to fresh, nutritious, and effortlessly delicious meals that capture the warm, inviting flavors of the Mediterranean. The beauty of Greek cooking is that the less-is-more approach means that none of these recipes require fancy equipment or painstaking technique. Simply seek out the best produce you can find and cook with what's in season.

These are classic homemade recipes prepared authentically, just as you might enjoy them in Greece. Begin with mezes, the enticing array of small savory dishes that set the stage for convivial gatherings. Then explore the world of savory pastries, where delicate dough meets the goodness of cheeses or vegetables become delectable patties and crispy fried balls. Discover the art of stuffed vegetables, where a bounty of fresh produce transforms into a comforting pot or pan of food. Complement your meals with a chapter of soups and side dishes brimming with vegetables, grains, and legumes. Delve into seafood mains with different preparation techniques and authentic chicken and meat dishes. And finally, indulge in a delightful selection of sweets, the perfect companions to drinks of all kinds.

Working on this cookbook was a joyous and exciting journey for me. I got to visit Greece more often than I usually do, cook with friends and family, research Greek cuisine, and experiment a lot in the kitchen to re-create the dishes I remember from my childhood. *Yassou* brings together the classic Greek food that everyone loves and that is closest to my heart.

I hope you will enjoy it as much as I do.

—*Shaily Lipa*

ONE

MEZES AND STARTERS

The word *meze* translates to "a bite" or "a taste," but the origins of the word are debated. Some say it made its way into the Greek lexicon from the Turkish language, although it is entirely possible that it is ancient Persian or even Italian. Either way, mezes are the real attraction in Greek cuisine, and the variety is endless.

These small to medium dishes can range from simple vegetables and salads to dips and cheeses to savory pastries and fried bites.

Mezes are the messengers of appetite; the Greeks say that even if you're not hungry, the desire to nibble on something will arrive the moment they are brought to the table. The rich and beautiful meze spread is deeply rooted in Greek culture, in which eating together is a significant and beloved part of social life. The mezes are served in the center of the table, oftentimes alongside alcoholic drinks. When a party of Greeks enjoy mezes, they are sure to talk, laugh, and sometimes sing, dance, and invite other people to join them, while more and more plates are piled up and more drinks are poured.

The ingredients in meze dishes tend to be seasonal, and they are treated with minimal fuss, the key word being *simplicity*. The simplest of meze dishes are fresh vegetables and cheeses, such as salted tomato wedges or sliced feta sprinkled with dried oregano, but the best-known are the classic Greek Salad (page 39)—which features the beloved ingredients of tomatoes, cucumbers, bell peppers, olives, and cheese—and Tzatziki (page 25), a yogurt-based dip that contains shredded cucumber, garlic, and fresh dill. There are also many salads of roasted or boiled vegetables, such as Braised Leeks (page 44) and White Beans Baked in Tomato Sauce (page 50), that make great options for vegetarians and vegans. Seafood lovers won't be left out, either, with dishes like Fried Squid (page 61) and Grilled Octopus (page 62).

Each dish stands on its own and can also be part of almost any type of meal. However, if you want to create a whole classic Greek meze table, you should make about two spreads; a salad of fresh vegetables; one or two dishes of boiled, baked, or fried vegetables; and some kind of seafood dish; all alongside feta, of course, or another fresh, baked, or fried cheese.

22
EGGPLANT SPREAD
MELITZANOSALATA

25
YOGURT CUCUMBER DIP
TZATZIKI

26
SPLIT PEA SPREAD
FAVA

28
SPICY CHEESE DIP
TIROKAFTERI

29
GARLIC SPREAD
SKORDALIA

31
FISH ROE SPREAD
TARAMOSALATA

32
FRIED ZUCCHINI
KOLOKITHAKIA TIGANITA

33
ROASTED PEPPERS
PIPERIES FLORINIS

34
GREEK BRUSCHETTA
DAKOS

39
GREEK SALAD
HORIATIKI SALATA

40
BEET AND YOGURT SALAD
PANTZAROSALATA

44
BRAISED LEEKS
SALATA PRASSA

47
POTATO SALAD
PATATOSALATA

49
WHITE BEAN SALAD
FASSOLIA PIAZ

50
WHITE BEANS
BAKED IN TOMATO SAUCE
GIGANTES PLAKI

55
BAKED FETA
FETA PSITI

56
FETA IN CRISPY PHYLLO PASTRY
FETA ME MELI

59
FRIED CHEESE
SAGANAKI

61
FRIED SQUID
KALAMARIA TIGANITA

62
GRILLED OCTOPUS
OKTAPODI STA KARVOUNA

67
SHRIMP IN OLIVE OIL
GARIDES SE ELAIOLADO

68
SHRIMP SAGANAKI
GARIDES SAGANAKI

Eggplant Spread

MELITZANOSALATA

Makes about 1¼ cups (300 g)

2 medium Italian or globe eggplants, skin on

1 scallion (white and light green parts only), thinly sliced

2 or 3 garlic cloves, minced or grated

1 teaspoon lemon zest

3 to 4 tablespoons lemon juice

2 tablespoons extra-virgin olive oil

3 tablespoons finely chopped fresh flat-leaf parsley

½ to 1 teaspoon dried chili flakes (optional)

Kosher salt and freshly ground black pepper to taste

To serve

1 tablespoon extra-virgin olive oil

Pita or bread (optional)

The Greeks consider this dish a salad, but its consistency is much more akin to a spread. There are dozens of variations on melitzanosalata in Balkan cuisine, but this version is authentically Greek. Roasting the eggplant over an open fire makes all the difference in this recipe, giving the salad its characteristic deep charred flavor. The roasted eggplant is then chopped by hand (never in a food processor!) to retain a chunky texture, ensuring that every bite has a slightly different mouthfeel than the one before.

To char on a gas stovetop: Wrap each eggplant in aluminum foil. Char each eggplant on a separate burner over high heat, using tongs to turn it every 5 minutes or so, until the eggplants are very soft and the skin that sticks out from under the torn foil is blackened and blistered on all sides, 25 to 30 minutes total.

To char under the broiler: Line a sheet pan with aluminum foil and place parchment paper on top. Arrange the 2 eggplants on the pan and place them as close to the broiler as you can without the eggplants touching the heating element. Broil the eggplants, using tongs to turn them every 5 minutes or so, until the eggplants are tender and the skin is charred and blackened, 25 to 30 minutes total.

Let the eggplants rest (in the foil if using the stovetop method, or on the pan for the broiler method) until they are cool enough to handle, about 20 minutes.

Slice the eggplants in half lengthwise and scoop out the flesh. Discard the skins. Place the flesh in a fine-mesh sieve and allow any juices to drain, about 20 minutes.

Remove the eggplant flesh from the sieve, roughly chop it, and transfer to a medium bowl. Add the scallion, garlic, lemon zest, 3 tablespoons lemon juice, the 2 tablespoons olive oil, the parsley, chili flakes (if using), salt, and pepper, and mix.

Transfer to an airtight container and refrigerate for at least 2 hours to let the flavors combine.

Taste and adjust the seasoning. Add more lemon juice, if needed.

Spread the melitzanosalata on a serving plate and drizzle with the 1 tablespoon olive oil. Serve immediately with pita, if desired.

Leftover melitzanosalata can be stored in an airtight container in the refrigerator for up to 4 days.

MIGHTY EGGPLANT

The eggplant is probably the most beloved vegetable in Greek cuisine. Eggplant can be intimidating to cook with for those who are not used to it, but the preparation is actually quite simple. This nightshade is incredibly versatile and can be prepared in many ways.

- Choose a shiny, taut eggplant with a fresh green stalk. The weight of the eggplant should be relatively light. Small and medium eggplants have more flavor. If you can find them, use the heirloom variety called baladi; they have a mild, slightly sweet flavor and a creamy texture.

- Roasting a whole eggplant produces a deep smoky flavor that is typically sought out in eggplant dishes such as the meze spread Melitzanosalata. Before roasting the eggplant on the grill or over a stovetop burner, wrap it in aluminum foil, which helps prevent some of the liquid from escaping. Don't prick the eggplant before placing it on the grill or flame.

- Frying or baking slices of eggplant creates a crispy texture that will distinguish the eggplant from the other ingredients in a dish, as in Moussaka (page 211), for example. If you aren't up for frying, you can roast eggplant in the oven, drizzled with olive oil, which is less messy and uses less oil but produces a similar taste. Since eggplants contain mostly water, you may need to sweat your eggplant by sprinkling salt on sliced rounds in order to draw out some of its liquid. If the eggplant is very fresh, you can skip this step and fry or bake immediately after slicing without salting the eggplant rounds.

Yogurt Cucumber Dip

TZATZIKI

Makes about 3 cups (600 g)

2 medium Persian cucumbers, skin on

2 cups (480 g) full-fat Greek yogurt

2 or 3 garlic cloves, minced or grated

2 tablespoons finely chopped fresh dill

2 tablespoons finely chopped fresh mint

2 tablespoons extra-virgin olive oil

Kosher salt and freshly ground black pepper to taste

To serve

1 tablespoon extra-virgin olive oil

Pita or bread (optional)

Just three primary ingredients—thick yogurt, grated cucumbers, and crushed garlic—make up one of Greece's most popular dishes. Tzatziki is ubiquitous in Greek cuisine and is enjoyed as a meze with pita or bread, a dip for vegetables, a sauce for patties and meatballs, or a topping for main dishes like souvlaki and gyros. Its flavors develop and deepen over time, so it's worth making at least two hours ahead. Use thick, rich Greek yogurt and you won't need to drain the liquid with a cheesecloth. There are many versions of tzatziki, but this is the winning classic.

Trim the ends of the cucumbers. Using the large holes of a box grater, grate the cucumbers (be careful of your fingertips!).

Squeeze the liquid from the grated cucumbers with your hands, working one handful at a time, or place all the grated cucumbers in a cheesecloth bag and wring out the liquid. Transfer the squeezed cucumbers to a medium bowl. Add the yogurt, garlic, dill, mint, the 2 tablespoons olive oil, and the salt and pepper, and mix.

Transfer to an airtight container and refrigerate for at least 2 hours to let the flavors combine.

Taste and adjust the seasoning, if needed.

Spread the tzatziki on a serving plate and drizzle with the 1 tablespoon olive oil. Serve immediately with pita, if desired.

Leftover tzatziki can be stored in an airtight container in the refrigerator for up to 4 days.

Split Pea Spread

FAVA

Makes about 2¾ cups (550 g)

1 cup (180 g) dried yellow split peas

1 medium onion, cut into quarters

3 garlic cloves, smashed

¼ cup (60 ml) extra-virgin olive oil

3 tablespoons lemon juice

Kosher salt and freshly ground black pepper to taste

To serve

1 tablespoon extra-virgin olive oil

½ small red onion, finely chopped (optional)

1 teaspoon small capers (optional)

Pita or bread (optional)

Originally, this Greek spread called fava (which is similar to hummus) was made out of fava beans—hence its name. With time, the beans were replaced with dried yellow split peas grown in Santorini, considered the best of their kind because of the island's volcanic soil. The peas are rich in plant-based protein, nutritious fiber, vitamins, minerals, and antioxidants. If you buy the dried peas in a sealed package, choose one with an expiration date as far out as possible, and if you buy the peas in bulk, be sure there is high turnover at the store. The cooking time for dried peas that aren't fresh is much longer, and they have an off-putting aftertaste.

Rinse the peas under cold water in a fine-mesh sieve until the water runs clear, and drain.

Transfer the peas to a medium pot, pour in 2½ quarts (2½ L) cold water, and add the onion and garlic. Bring to a boil over high heat, reduce the heat to low, and simmer uncovered for 60 to 90 minutes, until the peas are fully tender. Use a slotted spoon to skim off the foam as the peas are cooking. Reserve ¾ cup (180 ml) of the cooking liquid and then drain the pot through a fine-mesh sieve.

Let the peas, onion, and garlic cool slightly, about 10 minutes.

Transfer the peas, onion, and garlic to the bowl of a food processor along with ¼ cup (60 ml) of the reserved cooking liquid. Add the ¼ cup (60 ml) olive oil, the lemon juice, salt, and pepper and process until smooth, about 2 minutes, stopping to scrape down the sides of the bowl if necessary. If the spread is too thick, add 2 to 3 more tablespoons of the cooking liquid and puree until creamy and smooth. Taste and adjust the seasoning, if needed.

Spread the fava on a plate. Drizzle with the 1 tablespoon olive oil and sprinkle with the red onion and capers, if desired. Serve immediately warm or at room temperature, with pita, if desired.

Leftover fava can be stored in an airtight container in the refrigerator for up to 3 days. The fava will thicken when chilled. Add 2 to 3 tablespoons of warm water and mix to bring it to the desired thickness and temperature.

Greek Salad

HORIATIKI SALATA

Serves 4 to 6

⅓ cup (80 ml) extra-virgin olive oil

3 tablespoons red wine vinegar

¾ teaspoon kosher salt, plus more to taste

¼ teaspoon freshly ground black pepper, plus more to taste

1 small red onion, halved and thinly sliced

4 ripe but firm medium heirloom tomatoes or 5 Roma tomatoes, cut into 1-inch (2.5 cm) chunks (see Notes)

2 medium Persian cucumbers, peeled and cut into ¼-inch (6 mm) rounds

1 medium green bell pepper, halved, cored, seeded, and cut into 1-inch (2.5 cm) chunks

½ cup (80 g) Kalamata olives, with pits

1 to 2 tablespoons capers (optional)

One 5-ounce (140 g) slice feta, cut ⅔ inch (1.7 cm) thick

To serve

1 teaspoon dried oregano

1 tablespoon extra-virgin olive oil

Bread or pita (optional)

This salad, which contains all the rich treasures of the Mediterranean summer, is deserving of its star status. You can find a Greek salad in almost every taverna and restaurant throughout the country, though the *horiatiki* in the name comes from the Greek word *horio,* meaning "village." Greeks have been making similar salads since the early 1800s, but it wasn't until the 1960s that feta was incorporated and the modern Greek salad was born. At the time, taverna owners from the Plaka neighborhood of Athens were looking for a way to bypass the fixed prices for salads set by the government. Adding a block of feta on top technically moved the dish into a category for which the law allowed taverna owners to set their own prices.

These days, you will find this salad made with different varieties of tomato, but the key is to use perfectly ripe, high-quality tomatoes. If you can't find ripe, juicy tomatoes, it's best to make Greek salad at another time. In Greece, this salad is always served with bread to mop up all the juices, a practice called *papara.*

In a large bowl, whisk together the ⅓ cup (80 ml) olive oil, vinegar, salt, and black pepper. Add the onion and mix. Let sit until the onion begins to soften, about 20 minutes.

Add the tomatoes, cucumbers, bell pepper, olives, and capers (if using) to the bowl, and toss to coat the salad in the dressing.

Taste and adjust the seasoning, if needed.

Arrange the salad in a serving bowl and place the feta on top. Sprinkle the cheese with the oregano and drizzle with the 1 tablespoon olive oil. Serve immediately with bread, if desired.

Notes

- If you can't find sweet heirloom or Roma tomatoes, use 25 sweet cherry tomatoes, halved.

- The pickled onion can be made up to 2 days ahead, stored in an airtight container, and refrigerated. It's also great for sandwiches.

Beet and Yogurt Salad

PANTZAROSALATA

Serves 4 to 6

4 medium beets, skin on, scrubbed well

1 heaping tablespoon kosher salt, plus more to taste

1 cup (240 g) full-fat Greek yogurt

¼ cup (60 ml) extra-virgin olive oil

2 teaspoons white wine vinegar

2 tablespoons lemon juice

2 or 3 garlic cloves, minced or grated

Freshly ground black pepper to taste

To serve

½ cup (60 g) coarsely chopped raw walnuts

Sweet beets cooked until tender, then diced, enveloped in a velvety yogurt sauce, and garnished with crunchy, earthy walnuts. This salad can be part of your meze spread or is an excellent accompaniment to main dishes, especially fish. You can prepare it ahead of time and store it in the refrigerator, but take it out about 30 minutes before serving so it won't be too cold. It's best to use medium-sized beets, which have a deeper, more concentrated flavor than large ones.

Place the beets in a medium pot. Add the salt and enough water to cover the beets by 2 inches (5 cm). Bring to a boil over high heat, reduce the heat to low, and simmer uncovered for 50 to 60 minutes, until the beets are tender and a knife can easily pierce them.

Drain the beets and allow them to cool until lukewarm.

Use your hands to rub off the skins, and then cut the beets into ½-inch (12 mm) cubes. (You may want to wear disposable plastic or latex kitchen gloves to prevent your hands from staining when you do this.)

In a large bowl, whisk together the yogurt, olive oil, vinegar, lemon juice, garlic, salt, and pepper, until the dressing is smooth and velvety. Add the beet cubes and toss. Taste and adjust the seasoning, if needed.

Sprinkle with the walnuts. Serve immediately at room temperature.

Leftover pantzarosalata can be stored in an airtight container in the refrigerator for up to 3 days.

Braised Leeks

SALATA PRASSA

Serves 6 to 8

¼ cup (60 ml) extra-virgin
olive oil

1 medium onion, finely chopped

2 garlic cloves, finely chopped

2 cups (480 ml) water

¼ cup (60 ml) lemon juice

½ teaspoon sugar

Kosher salt and freshly ground
black pepper to taste

4 medium or 5 small leeks,
cut into ¾-inch (2 cm) rounds

While leeks often play a supporting role in Greek dishes, they are the star in this winter meze dish. The leeks are cooked in a flavorful liquid until they are tender and sweet. It is important to use fresh leeks for this recipe.

In a large nonstick pan, heat the olive oil over medium heat. Add the onion and garlic and cook for 5 to 6 minutes, stirring occasionally, until the onion and garlic are soft and fragrant.

Add the water, lemon juice, sugar, salt, and pepper, and stir. Add the leeks and bring to a boil over high heat. Reduce the heat to medium-low and cook uncovered for 30 to 35 minutes, until the leeks are tender but not mushy. Don't stir the leeks while they cook, just turn them over halfway through cooking, using tongs, so the rounds keep their shape. Taste and adjust the seasoning, if needed.

Serve at room temperature or cold.

Leftover salata prassa can be stored in an airtight container in the refrigerator for up to 4 days.

LEEKS Grown in Greece since antiquity, leeks were one of the major agricultural products during Byzantine times, and Greeks believe that the leek has medicinal powers. Cantors in the Greek Orthodox church traditionally drink the juice of boiled leeks to soften their voices.

When cooking with leeks, choose young, thin stalks, which are the juiciest and full of flavor. The thick ones tend to be more fibrous, with a woody and inedible inner part. Look for leeks with a whole bulb, neither cracked nor bruised, and with green leaves on top. Fresh leeks should be shiny, straight, and firm and resist being bent.

Leeks often have sand or dirt tucked between the layers. To clean them, put the cut leeks in a large bowl, cover with plenty of water, and let soak for 20 minutes. The sand will sink to the bottom and the leeks will float on top. Then use your hands or a slotted spoon to lift the leeks out of the water and transfer them to a colander. Do not tip the leeks directly from the bowl into the colander. Rinse the leeks under running water for about a minute until the water runs clear.

Potato Salad

PATATOSALATA

Serves 4 to 6

6 medium waxy potatoes, peeled and cut into 6 chunks each

1 heaping tablespoon kosher salt, plus more to taste

⅓ cup (80 ml) extra-virgin olive oil

1 teaspoon lemon zest

2 tablespoons lemon juice

2 tablespoons white wine vinegar

1 heaping teaspoon whole-grain Dijon mustard

1 heaping teaspoon honey

Freshly ground black pepper to taste

1 small red onion, finely chopped

⅓ cup (45 g) halved and pitted Kalamata olives

3 tablespoons finely chopped fresh flat-leaf parsley

1 heaping tablespoon small capers

The Ottoman Empire brought potatoes to Greece by the fifteenth century. At the time, though, they were received with skepticism by the Greek Orthodox priests, who claimed they were the apple that Eve gave to Adam in the Garden of Eden, and therefore eating them was a sin. Only with the arrival of the English in southern Greece at the end of the eighteenth century did potatoes become a respectable part of the Greek menu. Since then, the Greeks have come to love them and use them as a base for dips and sauces, add them to Moussaka (page 211) and casseroles, grill them alongside chicken, lamb, and more. There is no mayonnaise or sour cream in Greek potato salad, but rather a delicate mix of olive oil, lemon zest, lemon juice, vinegar, mustard, and honey. The red onion, olives, and capers add flavor and bite.

Place the potatoes in a medium pot. Add the salt and enough water to cover the potatoes by 2 inches (5 cm). Bring to a boil over high heat, reduce the heat to low, and simmer uncovered for 15 to 20 minutes, until the potatoes are tender but not mushy.

Drain the potatoes and allow them to cool until lukewarm.

In a large bowl, whisk together the olive oil, lemon zest, lemon juice, vinegar, mustard, honey, salt, and pepper. Add the potatoes, onion, olives, parsley, and capers, and toss. Taste and adjust the seasoning, if needed.

Serve immediately at room temperature.

Leftover patatosalata can be stored in an airtight container in the refrigerator for up to 4 days.

White Bean Salad

FASSOLIA PIAZ

Serves 6 to 8

2 cups (340 g) dried white beans, preferably cannellini or navy beans, soaked in water overnight or for at least 8 hours

1 medium red onion, finely chopped

½ cup finely chopped fresh flat-leaf parsley

⅓ cup (80 ml) extra-virgin olive oil

¼ cup (60 ml) white wine vinegar

3 tablespoons lemon juice

Kosher salt and freshly ground black pepper to taste

Every cook in the Balkans makes a white bean salad, but this recipe comes from my Greek grandmother, Levana, who made it every Sabbath for the glorious Greek breakfasts we ate with her and my grandfather on their balcony. Her version is simply seasoned with olive oil and vinegar. I also like to add lemon juice, which gives the salad a different facet of acidity.

The beans must soak in water overnight or for at least 8 hours, so be sure to plan ahead.

Rinse the soaked beans in a colander under cold water until the water runs clear, and drain.

Transfer the beans to a large pot and cover with 5 quarts (5 L) of cold water. Bring to a boil over high heat, reduce the heat to low, and simmer uncovered for 90 to 120 minutes, until the beans are fully tender. Use a slotted spoon to skim off the foam as the beans are cooking. Drain the beans and allow them to cool until lukewarm.

Transfer the beans to a large bowl. Add the onion, parsley, olive oil, vinegar, lemon juice, salt, and pepper, and toss. Taste and adjust the seasoning, if needed.

Serve at room temperature.

Leftover fassolia piaz can be stored in an airtight container in the refrigerator for up to 4 days.

White Beans Baked in Tomato Sauce

GIGANTES PLAKI

Serves 6 to 8

2 cups (320 g) dried large white beans, preferably gigantes, lima, or butter beans, soaked in water overnight or for at least 8 hours

⅓ cup (80 ml) extra-virgin olive oil

1 large onion, finely chopped

1 large carrot, cut into ¼-inch (6 mm) cubes

2 celery stalks, cut into ¼-inch (6 mm) cubes

2 or 3 garlic cloves, finely chopped

3 tablespoons finely chopped fresh flat-leaf parsley

2 tablespoons finely chopped fresh mint

2 tablespoons finely chopped fresh dill

1 teaspoon dried oregano

¼ to ½ teaspoon chili flakes

3 tablespoons tomato paste

One 14-ounce (400 g) can crushed tomatoes

2½ cups (600 ml) warm water

2 or 3 bay leaves

Kosher salt and freshly ground black pepper to taste

Cherry tomatoes on the vine (optional)

In the Greek diet, beans are an excellent source of plant-based protein, especially during the many religious fasts throughout the year, when those adhering to the Greek Orthodox fasting calendar avoid meat. This dish can be served as part of a table of mezes, but it can also be used as a wonderful vegan main course. The word *gigantes* means "giant" in Greek, and it refers to large white beans reminiscent of butter beans in the United States, but a little firmer and larger. *Plaki* refers to the cooking method used: It means baked in the oven in tomato sauce with onion, garlic, and parsley.

The beans must soak in water overnight or for at least 8 hours, so be sure to plan ahead.

Rinse the soaked beans in a colander under cold water until the water runs clear, and drain.

Transfer the beans to a large pot and cover with 5 quarts (5 L) of cold water. Bring to a boil over high heat, reduce the heat to low, and simmer uncovered for 90 to 120 minutes, until the beans are fully tender. Use a slotted spoon to skim off the foam as the beans are cooking. Drain the beans and set aside.

Preheat the oven to 350°F (175°C).

In a large nonstick pan, heat the ⅓ cup (80 ml) olive oil over medium heat. Add the onion, carrot, celery, and garlic, and cook for 6 to 8 minutes, stirring occasionally, until the vegetables are soft and fragrant. Add the 3 tablespoons parsley, the mint, dill, oregano, and chili flakes, and sauté for 1 minute.

Add the tomato paste and sauté for another minute. Add the crushed tomatoes, water, cooked beans, bay leaves, salt, and pepper. Stir well and bring to a boil. Taste and adjust the seasoning, if needed.

Carefully pour the bean mixture into a 9-by-13-inch (23 by 33 cm) baking dish. Place the cherry tomato cluster on top, if desired.

(ingredients continue)

(recipe continues)

To serve

2 tablespoons extra-virgin olive oil

2 tablespoons finely chopped fresh flat-leaf parsley (optional)

Pita or bread (optional)

Bake uncovered for 40 to 45 minutes, until the beans are tender and bubbling and the top layer is golden brown. Halfway through cooking, check to see if the beans look dry and add a little more water if needed.

Remove the dish from the oven and remove and discard the bay leaves. Drizzle with the 2 tablespoons olive oil and sprinkle with the 2 tablespoons parsley, if you'd like.

Serve immediately with pita, if desired.

Leftover gigantes plaki can be stored in an airtight container in the refrigerator for up to 4 days. To reheat, warm in the oven at 325°F (160°C) for 8 to 10 minutes.

Baked Feta

FETA PSITI

Serves 6 to 8

10 ounces (280 g) feta, sliced ⅔ inch (1.7 cm) thick

35 cherry tomatoes (approximately 2 pints), halved

1 cup (130 g drained) quartered artichoke hearts marinated in olive oil (optional)

½ cup (80 g) pitted Kalamata olives

4 tablespoons (60 ml) extra-virgin olive oil

1¼ teaspoons dried oregano

Kosher salt and freshly ground black pepper to taste

To serve

Pita or bread (optional)

This is my twist on one of the best-known mezes in Greece. In its classic preparation, a block of feta is placed atop several thin slices of tomato, sprinkled with dried oregano and sometimes chili flakes, drizzled with olive oil, wrapped in foil, and baked in the oven. Here the dish is turned into a dreamy one-pan meal. Cherry tomatoes in a variety of colors meet the addition of artichokes and Kalamata olives, and the seasoned mixture surrounds blocks of melty feta. After your cheese spends some time in the oven, all you need is bread to mop up the sauce. When I have vegan guests, I swap out the feta for thin slices of high-quality tofu. This recipe is not purely Greek, but it's exceptional nonetheless.

Preheat the oven to 375°F (190°C).

Place the feta slices in the center of a 9-by-13-inch (23 by 33 cm) baking dish.

In a large bowl, toss the tomatoes, artichoke hearts (if using), olives, 3 tablespoons of the olive oil, 1 teaspoon of the oregano, and the salt and pepper. Taste and adjust the seasoning, if needed.

Arrange the tomato mixture around the feta. Drizzle the feta with the remaining 1 tablespoon olive oil and sprinkle with the remaining ¼ teaspoon oregano.

Bake uncovered for 35 to 45 minutes, until the feta is soft and golden. Serve immediately with pita, if desired.

Leftover feta psiti can be stored in an airtight container in the refrigerator for up to 4 days. To reheat, warm in the oven at 325°F (160°C) for 8 to 10 minutes.

Feta in Crispy Phyllo Pastry

FETA ME MELI

Serves 2 to 4

One 4-ounce (115 g) slice feta,
½ inch (12 mm) thick

2 sheets phyllo dough, thawed
overnight in the refrigerator
if frozen

2 tablespoons extra-virgin
olive oil

1 tablespoon white or black
sesame seeds (or both)

2 to 3 tablespoons honey

This traditional appetizer is easy to make and a perfect blend of flavors and textures: creamy feta wrapped in crispy phyllo leaves and topped with nutty sesame seeds. Honey is drizzled on top and provides a sweet contrast to the salinity of the feta and the crunch of the phyllo dough.

Preheat the oven to 350°F (175°C). Line a baking sheet with parchment paper.

Pat the feta block dry with a paper towel.

On a clean work surface, stack the 2 phyllo sheets, the short end toward you, and brush the top sheet with a little olive oil.

Place the feta horizontally in the center of the lower third of the phyllo sheet. Fold the bottom of the phyllo over the feta, then fold the sides and continue to wrap the phyllo around the feta, moving the cheese away from you, until you get a phyllo parcel.

Place the phyllo parcel on the prepared baking sheet seam-side down. Brush the top and sides with a little olive oil and sprinkle the sesame seeds on top.

Bake for 20 to 25 minutes, until the phyllo parcel is golden brown.

Drizzle with honey and serve immediately.

FETA Feta is the most popular cheese in Greece. It's made from sheep's milk or a combination of sheep's and goat's milk, formed into blocks, and stored in brine (salt water). The brine protects the cheese from exposure to air and keeps it fresh for up to 3 months. The flavor and creaminess of feta can vary depending on the personal preferences of the cheesemaker, the season, and the nutrition of the herd. It can be lightly salted or more heavily salted and can be made with a crumbly, creamy, or airy texture. When buying feta, look for a block in a container with brine as opposed to the pre-crumbled or vacuum-sealed varieties. Always buy a feta with a high percentage of fat. This is not the time to count calories.

Fried Cheese

SAGANAKI

Serves 2 to 4

2 tablespoons all-purpose flour

One 4-ounce (115 g) slice
kefalotyri or graviera,
½ inch (12 mm) thick

¼ to ⅓ cup (60 to 80 ml)
extra-virgin olive oil

To serve

½ lemon, cut into wedges

Pita or bread (optional)

Saganaki is the name of a type of heavy two-handled pan, usually made of copper and used to fry or cook individual portions of cheese, seafood, or meat. The traditional preparation of this dish is to fry cubes of semihard yellow cheese until they develop a crisp golden skin on the outside and are soft and stringy inside. Instead, in this recipe you fry a large slice of cheese, which is a quicker and easier process. It's best to use kefalotyri or graviera, both of which have a delicate nutty flavor. Kefalotyri maintains its shape especially well during the frying process, and it has a concentrated flavor similar to Parmesan. If you cannot find these two cheeses, halloumi, provolone, or even a young pecorino will work.

Place the flour in a shallow bowl. Dredge the cheese slice in the flour, coating it well, and shake off any excess flour. Set aside on a clean plate.

Cover the bottom of a small nonstick pan with olive oil about ¼ inch (6 mm) deep, and bring to a frying temperature over medium-high heat. You can check the temperature of the oil by dipping the handle of a wooden spoon in it. When the oil is ready, it will gently sizzle and bubble up around the handle.

Fry the cheese for 1 to 2 minutes on each side, until golden.

Remove the cheese from the pan and place on a serving plate. Squeeze the lemon over the top and serve immediately, with pita, if desired.

Variation

For a gluten-free version: Instead of flour, use 2 tablespoons cornstarch.

Fried Squid

KALAMARIA TIGANITA

Serves 4 to 6

1 pound (450 g) small squid, tubes cut into ½-inch (12 mm) rounds, tentacles left whole

1¼ cups (155 g) all-purpose flour

1 teaspoon dried oregano

1 teaspoon kosher salt

½ teaspoon freshly ground black pepper

4 cups (960 ml) vegetable oil

To serve

½ lemon, cut into wedges

According to the fasting rules of the Greek Orthodox tradition, squid is considered a "bloodless" animal and can therefore be eaten during those days when all meat and fish is to be avoided. It's preferable to use fresh calamari for this recipe, but good-quality frozen calamari will also work. Just make sure to defrost it slowly, preferably overnight in the refrigerator. Fry the calamari relatively quickly, so the rounds don't become too rubbery.

Rinse the squid tubes and tentacles in a colander under cold water until the water runs clear, and drain. Pat dry with a paper towel. Set aside.

In a medium bowl, mix the flour, oregano, salt, and pepper.

Cover the bottom of a medium skillet with vegetable oil at least 3 inches (8 cm) deep, and bring to a frying temperature over medium-high heat. You can check the temperature of the oil by dipping the handle of a wooden spoon in it. When the oil is ready, it will gently sizzle and bubble up around the handle.

Line a plate with a paper towel.

Dredge about a third of the squid in the flour mixture, coating it well. Use your hands to transfer the squid to a fine-mesh sieve to shake off any excess flour.

Drop the coated squid pieces into the oil and fry for 3 to 4 minutes, until golden. Using a slotted spoon, scoop the squid out and let drain on the paper towel–lined plate. Working in batches, repeat with the rest of the squid, a third at a time.

For extra crispiness, you can fry the squid for 2 to 3 minutes, until they start to turn golden, and let drain on the paper towel for 2 minutes. Return the fried squid to the oil for a second frying, and fry for 50 to 60 seconds over high heat, until golden brown.

Serve immediately with lemon wedges.

Variation

For a gluten-free version: Instead of flour, use 1¼ cups cornstarch.

Grilled Octopus

OKTAPODI STA KARVOUNA

Serves 4 to 6

1 medium octopus (1.2 kg), head and ink sac removed (800 g clean)

⅓ cup (80 ml) red wine vinegar

For the marinade

1 cup (240 ml) plus 3 tablespoons extra-virgin olive oil

½ cup (120 ml) dry red wine

1 tablespoon lemon zest

¼ cup (60 ml) lemon juice

2 or 3 garlic cloves, smashed

2 or 3 bay leaves

1 teaspoon dried oregano

¾ teaspoon kosher salt, plus more to taste

½ teaspoon freshly ground black pepper, plus more to taste

To serve

½ lemon, cut into wedges

No cookbook about Greek cuisine would be complete without a recipe for grilled octopus. The Greeks have loved octopus for thousands of years, and the sight of octopuses hung out to dry in the sun like freshly laundered clothes is very common along the coasts of Greece. Fishermen beat the catch of octopuses against the rocks of the shoreline to soften them up, then sell them to the fish markets or tavernas. In this recipe, the octopus is cooked in its own juices until tender, then marinated, and finally grilled. If you're not in a hurry, it's worth leaving the octopus to marinate overnight, so it can absorb as much flavor as possible. You can ask your fishmonger to remove the head and the ink sac from the octopus, if you prefer not to do it yourself.

Rinse the octopus in a colander under cold water until the water runs clear, and drain.

Use a large and sharp knife to separate the tentacles, drawing the knife from the center section out.

Place the whole octopus tentacles in a wide pot in one layer and add the vinegar. Bring to a boil over medium heat, reduce the heat to low, cover the pot, and simmer for 10 minutes. Remove the lid and check that the octopus has released liquid. It should be almost covered in its juices. If it did not release enough liquid, add 1 cup (240 ml) warm water and bring to a boil. Reduce the heat to low, re-cover the pot, and continue to simmer over low heat for another 40 to 50 minutes, until the octopus is fork-tender, using tongs to turn it over halfway through cooking. Drain well.

Prepare the marinade: In a large bowl, mix 1 cup (240 ml) of the olive oil, the wine, lemon zest, lemon juice, garlic, bay leaves, oregano, salt, and pepper. Add the cooked octopus and let rest for at least 1 hour. If you marinate it for longer than an hour, cover the bowl with plastic wrap and place it in the refrigerator. Remove the octopus from the refrigerator about 1 hour before grilling to bring it close to room temperature.

Heat a charcoal or gas grill over medium-high heat. Brush the grill with the remaining 3 tablespoons olive oil to prevent the octopus

from sticking. Lay the tentacles on the grill and cook for 3 to 4 minutes on each side, until the octopus is tender and slightly charred.

Remove the octopus from the grill, place on a serving plate, and squeeze the lemon on top. Taste and adjust the seasoning, adding salt and pepper if needed. Serve immediately.

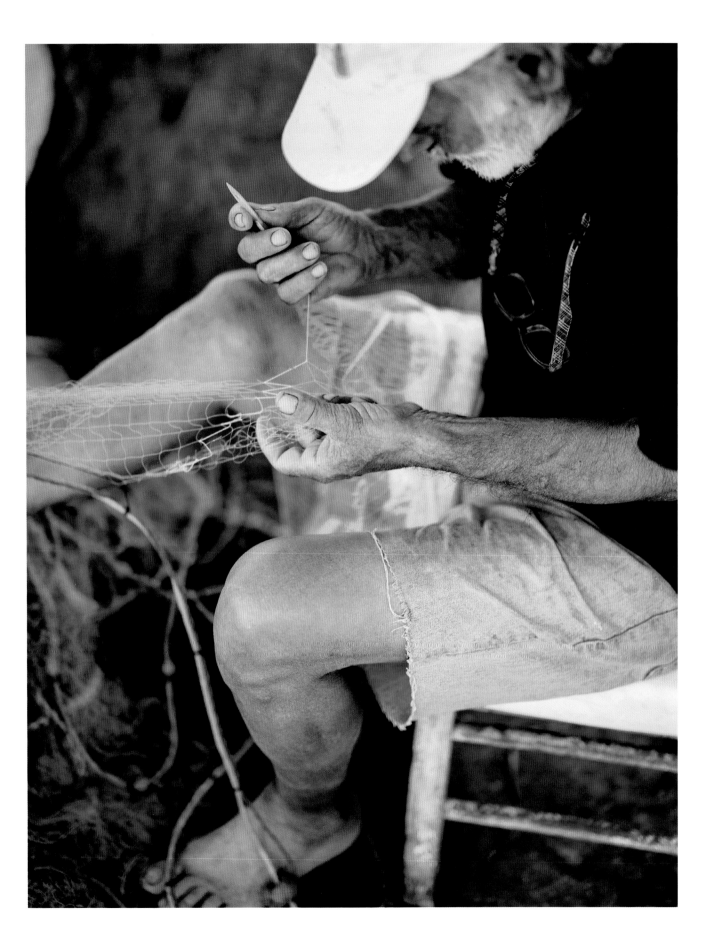

Shrimp in Olive Oil

GARIDES SE ELAIOLADO

Serves 4 to 6

1 pound (450 g) deveined tail-on medium shrimp

1 heaping tablespoon plus
1 heaping teaspoon kosher salt, plus more to taste

1¾ cups (420 ml) extra-virgin olive oil, plus more to taste

1¾ cups (420 ml) vegetable oil

1 medium lemon, cut into ¼-inch (6 mm) rounds

3 garlic cloves, thinly sliced

3 bay leaves

3 oregano sprigs

½ fresh red chili pepper, thinly sliced

½ teaspoon freshly ground black pepper, plus more to taste

To serve

½ lemon, cut into wedges

Pita or bread (optional)

Greece is surrounded by water, and a love for the sea permeates the culture of this country. Seafood is an important element in Greek cuisine, and the Greeks enjoy a bounty of it. This dish is an ode to one of its wonders: shrimp. Here lightly poached shrimp are soaked in a flavorful oil-based marinade. The shrimp can be cooked directly in the oil, but I think it's best to poach them in water first and then transfer them to the cold seasoned oil. That way, the cold liquid keeps the shrimp from overcooking, and they come out juicy in a fresh and clear oil.

Rinse the shrimp in a colander under cold water until the water runs clear, and drain.

Fill a large pot with water and season with 1 heaping tablespoon of the salt. Bring to a boil.

Add the shrimp and poach for exactly 1 minute, until the shrimp are bright pink and firm. Drain well and set aside.

In a large widemouthed jar or a large bowl, stir together the olive oil, vegetable oil, lemon rounds, garlic, bay leaves, oregano, chili pepper, the remaining 1 heaping teaspoon salt, and the black pepper. Add the poached shrimp and stir gently to coat all the shrimp in the marinade. If the shrimp are not completely covered, add more olive oil. Cover the jar and refrigerate for at least 4 hours to let the flavors combine.

Remove the shrimp from the oil, place on a serving plate, and squeeze the lemon on top.

Taste and adjust the seasoning, if needed. Serve with pita, if desired, to soak up the marinade.

Shrimp Saganaki

GARIDES SAGANAKI

Serves 4 to 6

1 pound (450 g) deveined tail-on medium shrimp

6 tablespoons (90 ml) extra-virgin olive oil

1 teaspoon lemon zest

2 tablespoons lemon juice

2 garlic cloves, minced or grated

½ teaspoon kosher salt, plus more to taste

¼ teaspoon freshly ground black pepper, plus more to taste

1 medium onion, finely chopped

One 14-ounce (400 g) can crushed tomatoes

¾ cup (180 ml) water

2 tablespoons ouzo

1 teaspoon dried oregano

½ to 1 teaspoon dried chili flakes (optional)

3 ounces (85 g) feta, coarsely crumbled

2 tablespoons finely chopped fresh flat-leaf parsley

To serve

Crusty bread (optional)

In this dish, shrimp are marinated in olive oil, garlic, and lemon and then cooked in a beautiful rich tomato sauce. I like to add a little ouzo to the sauce, which infuses it with the flavor of anise. Saganaki originally referred to a dish made with only cheese, and it is believed that shrimp saganaki was created in the 1960s to satisfy tourists who hankered for fresh seafood. Today shrimp saganaki is served in almost every taverna on the coast of Greece, along with plenty of crusty bread to soak up the sauce.

Rinse the shrimp in a colander under cold water until the water runs clear, and drain.

In a medium bowl, stir together 3 tablespoons of the olive oil, the lemon zest, lemon juice, garlic, ½ teaspoon salt, and ¼ teaspoon pepper. Add the shrimp and toss gently to coat all the shrimp with the marinade. Set aside.

In a medium nonstick skillet, heat the remaining 3 tablespoons olive oil over medium heat. Add the onion and cook for 5 to 6 minutes, stirring occasionally, until the onion is soft and fragrant.

Add the crushed tomatoes, water, ouzo, oregano, chili flakes (if using), and salt and pepper to taste, and mix. Bring to a boil over high heat, reduce the heat to low, and simmer uncovered for 15 to 20 minutes, until the sauce is rich and thick. Taste and adjust the seasoning, if needed.

Add the shrimp with their marinade, bring to a boil over medium-high heat, and cook for 2 to 3 minutes on each side, until the shrimp are cooked through.

Sprinkle the feta and the parsley on top and cook for 1 minute, until the feta is warm.

Serve immediately in the pan that the dish was cooked in, accompanied by crusty bread, if desired.

ΜΥΖΗΘΡΑ
ΞΥΝΗ
8€ /ΚΙΛΟ

Τυρο ζουλι
11 T. Κιλο

ΑΝΘΟΓΑΛΟ
8,50 € /ΚΙΛΟ

THE CHEESES OF GREECE

Cheese has been a staple of the Greek diet since before recorded history. Some of the earliest archaeological evidence for cheesemaking, such as clay cheese strainers and stone tablets depicting cheesemaking scenes, comes from the island of Crete and dates back eight thousand years. According to myth, Apollo, the god of music, poetry, and art, sent his son Aristaeus to teach humans beekeeping, olive cultivation, and cheesemaking. Apollo's brother Hermes was the patron god of cheesemakers and animal herders. The Greeks considered cheese a gift from the gods, and during major ceremonies they ritualistically offered cheeses back to the gods. Cheese-based sweets were used as wedding invitations, and gifts of roasted cheesecakes covered in honey were exchanged between the families of the bride and groom, while one of the celebrated stars of the ancient wedding table was the plakountas, a sweet cake made with fine flour and filled with cheese and honey.

During the Golden Age of Pericles, Athens had an entire section of its main market devoted to cheese products, while small cheese pies covered in sesame seeds and fried in olive oil were a favorite on-the-go food, much like cheese-pie slices in modern Greece. In Sparta, the rite of passage for young men into full adulthood involved hiding pieces of cheese around the city, while seasoned warriors were known to eat cheese before battle. In medieval times, cheeses from the mainland and the islands were popular throughout the Byzantine Empire, and cheese was a favorite breakfast for commoners and royalty alike.

Cheese has a central place at the Greek table today, accompanying almost every meal and enjoyed in a variety of forms: crumbled in salads, stuffed in vegetables, grilled whole, or mixed into spreads. The Greek Orthodox calendar even has an entire week devoted to its consumption. During the week before Lent, in preparation for the fasting that is to come, people turn away from meat and fish and toward cheese and a dairy-based diet. The Sunday before Lent is known as Cheese Sunday, and a multitude of local cheese delicacies are shared in festivals throughout the country. During the carnival festivities, cheese dishes are to be eaten before anything else.

Along with the French and the Italians, Greeks consume more cheese than any other European nation. The country is also among the top producers of cheese in the European Union, with hundreds of quality cheesemaking facilities, most of them family owned and operated, employing techniques passed down from generation to generation. Greece produces dozens of different kinds of cheese of all varieties—hard, semihard, soft, and spreadable.

The best known of the spreadable cheeses is kopanisti, a salty, spicy cheese produced in the Cyclades. It is traditionally enjoyed with a

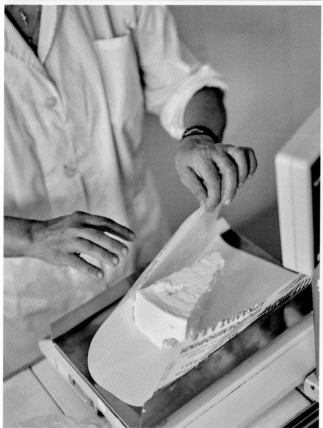
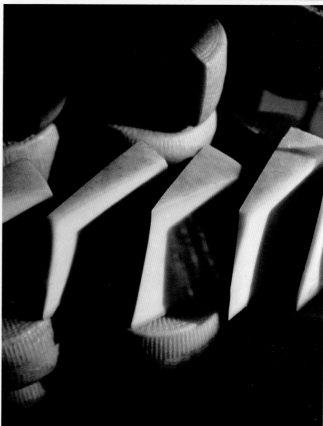

glass of ouzo and has a documented history going back more than three centuries. Low-salt soft cheeses—such as anthotiro ("flowery cheese"), a sweet white creamy cheese—are often eaten for breakfast topped with fruit and honey.

Manouri is a beloved semihard white cheese made from goat's or sheep's milk. It is creamier than feta, and because it has almost no salt, it is preferred for baking in pastries. Mizithra, a mixed milk-whey cheese made from sheep's or goat's milk or both, is another favorite semihard cheese; it is similar to Italian ricotta. Another popular semihard cheese is metsovone, a smoked cheese produced in the village of Metsovo in central Greece from cow's milk, although sometimes sheep's or goat's milk may be added. Cheeses made from cow's milk are rare, since the mountainous landscapes of the mainland do not lend themselves to cattle grazing.

Hard and semihard cheeses are typically grouped under the term *kasseri*, and some of the most famous are produced in the region of Epirus in central Greece. This includes the oldest of the hard cheeses, kefalotyri, a yellow-white salty and spicy cheese made from sheep's milk that Greeks love grating over pasta. In fact, one of the most popular cheeses in Greece is graviera, a hard sheep's milk cheese made in wheels. The rind of the cheese is marked with the characteristic crisscross pattern of its draining cloth.

The undisputed star of this great variety of cheeses is feta. The first recorded mention of it comes from Homer early in the first millennium BCE. In the *Odyssey*, Homer describes how the one-eyed giant Polyphemus discovered what is believed to be the ancestor of feta by accident. One day the Cyclops found that the milk from his sheep, which he stored in bags made from animal stomachs, had curdled and acquired a firm consistency and a tasty flavor. In fact, the word for cheese in Greek, *tiros* or *tiri*, literally means "curdled." The name *feta* is derived from the Greek word *pheta*, meaning "slice," and most likely refers to the practice of slicing up the blocks of cheese and placing them in wooden barrels or to the customary serving of the cheese in the form of thin slices. In the fifteenth century, Italian merchants began importing feta from Crete, but it wasn't until the early twentieth century—given impetus by Greek immigration to the United States, Northern Europe, and Australia, and by the advent of modern tourism—that feta became known outside the eastern Mediterranean. A century ago, the Greek government recognized feta as an original Greek product. Today feta is one of the most widely exported Greek products and the best-known of the twenty-one Greek cheeses classified by the European Commission as Protected Designation of Origin (PDO) products.

TWO

PATTIES AND SAVORY PASTRIES

Since antiquity, Greek cuisine has paid a great deal of respect to vegetables, cheeses, meats, and doughs, combining them into many kinds of patties and pastries—both individual and family sized. Greek pastries come in many shapes—

rectangles, circles, spirals, and triangles—and are sometimes made to look like cigars or boats. Some are baked in pans that define the edges of the pastry; others feature a dough shaped around a filling. Sometimes the mixture is shaped into balls or flattened into patties and fried, and sometimes it's a pastry in a baking dish comprising several layers.

The Greeks buy their pastries fresh from street vendors, who keep them warm under the lights of their carts, or from neighborhood bakeries, where the work of baking begins in the wee hours of the morning, before the sun rises. Almost every street has its own bakery, and you can catch a whiff of freshly baked pastries even in dense urban settings. Customers often have long-established relationships with the bakers, and most bakeries are family businesses that have been passed down from parent to child for generations.

There were many sweet and savory pies in ancient Greek cuisine. During the Byzantine and Ottoman periods, pies played a central role in Greek diet and culture. Today pies are still a part of the everyday diet, often enjoyed by workers in the cities, on the go in the fields or pastures, or on the road. There are even eateries devoted just to pies, called tiropitadika, that sell both savory and sweet pies to go. Pies often act as a whole meal but are also part of the spread for major holidays and are shared with friends and relatives at festive occasions.

In the United States, the word *pita* often refers to the Greek flatbread, but *pita* is actually translated as "pie." The term refers to pastries often made of phyllo dough, like the famous Spanakopita (page 97), or sometimes puff pastry (pâte feuilletée)—an ingredient imported from France—as in the Potato Pastry Rolls (page 95). Preparing phyllo or pastry dough from scratch requires specialized skills and more than a little time, but luckily, prepared doughs are readily available in supermarkets. Store-bought phyllo is excellent, and when it's used, all that's left to do is to make the fillings. All the recipes in this chapter recommend using store-bought dough.

Fried Zucchini and Feta Balls

KOLOKITHOKEFTEDES

Makes about 20 croquettes

3 medium zucchini

5 ounces (140 g) feta, coarsely crumbled

1 large egg

½ cup (50 g) plus 2 tablespoons bread crumbs

2 scallions (white and light green parts only), thinly sliced

2 tablespoons finely chopped fresh flat-leaf parsley

2 tablespoons finely chopped fresh mint

1 tablespoon lemon zest

½ teaspoon freshly ground black pepper, plus more to taste

¼ teaspoon kosher salt

4 cups (960 ml) vegetable oil

To serve

½ lemon, cut into wedges (optional)

Tzatziki (page 25; optional)

This is the Greek vegetarian version of meatballs. Zucchini fritters are a taste of summer and a delicacy with many variations throughout the country. The secret is to drain the grated zucchini well before adding them to the rest of the ingredients. This will make the balls stable enough to work with and will prevent them from falling apart while they are frying, plus the outside will be crispier and more delicious, too. Serve them as an appetizer with tzatziki or tomato sauce or as part of a table of mezes.

Trim the ends of the zucchini. Using the large holes of a box grater, grate the zucchini (be careful of your fingertips!).

Squeeze the water from the grated zucchini with your hands, working one handful at a time, or place all the grated zucchini in a cheesecloth bag and wring out the liquid. Transfer the zucchini to a large bowl. Add the feta, egg, 2 tablespoons of the bread crumbs, the scallions, parsley, mint, lemon zest, and pepper, and mix.

Do a taste test. In a small pan with a little oil, fry a tiny portion of the zucchini mixture. Taste and adjust the seasoning, if needed.

In a separate medium bowl, mix the remaining ½ cup (50 g) bread crumbs and the salt.

Moisten your hands with a little water to keep the mixture from sticking to them. Use your hands to scoop out about a flat tablespoon of the zucchini mixture and shape it into a 1½-inch (4 cm) ball. Roll it in the bread crumbs. Place the ball on a plate or a tray. Repeat until you have used up all the zucchini mixture.

Cover a medium skillet with the vegetable oil at least 3 inches (8 cm) deep, and bring to a frying temperature over medium-high heat. You can check the temperature of the oil by dipping the handle of a wooden spoon in it. When the oil is ready, it will gently sizzle and bubble up around the handle.

Line a plate with a paper towel.

(recipe continues)

Tomato Sauce

Makes about ½ cup (120 ml)

2 medium heirloom tomatoes
or 3 tomatoes on the vine,
halved horizontally

1 to 2 tablespoons extra-virgin
olive oil

¼ teaspoon dried oregano
(optional)

Kosher salt and freshly ground
black pepper to taste

This sauce goes perfectly with any patty or savory pie, and is also great to serve with pita or crusty bread.

Using the large holes of a box grater, grate the tomatoes with the cut side facing the grater until only the skin of the tomato remains (be careful of your fingertips!). Discard the skin.

Transfer the grated tomatoes to a small bowl. Add the olive oil, oregano (if using), salt, and pepper.

Taste and adjust the seasoning, if needed.

Santorini Tomato Patties

TOMATOKEFTEDES SANTORINIS

Makes about 12 patties

5 medium heirloom tomatoes or 8 tomatoes on the vine, halved horizontally

1 small red onion, finely chopped

1 scallion (white and light green parts only), thinly sliced

3 tablespoons finely chopped fresh flat-leaf parsley

2 tablespoons finely chopped fresh basil

¾ teaspoon kosher salt, plus more to taste

½ teaspoon freshly ground black pepper, plus more to taste

1¼ cups (155 g) all-purpose flour

1 teaspoon baking powder

¾ cup (180 ml) extra-virgin olive oil

To serve
Tzatziki (page 25; optional)

These vegan summer patties may have originated in Santorini, but today they are served all over Greece. Slightly overripe tomatoes, ones no longer suitable for salads, get mixed with other staple ingredients available in every household, such as onion and flour. The result is greater than the sum of its parts, which is why tomatokeftedes are also called "poor man's meatballs."

Using a teaspoon, scoop out the tomato seeds. Discard the seeds.

Chop the tomatoes into 1-inch (2.5 cm) chunks and transfer to a large bowl. Add the onion, scallion, parsley, basil, salt, and pepper, and knead with one hand for about 1 minute, until the mixture gains a pulpy texture.

In a separate bowl, stir together the flour and baking powder.

Add the flour mixture to the tomato mixture and mix. Let rest for 10 minutes.

Do a taste test. In a small pan with a little oil, fry a tiny portion of the tomato mixture. Taste and adjust the seasoning, if needed.

Moisten your hands with a little water to keep the mixture from sticking to them. Use your hands to scoop out about a heaping tablespoon of the tomato mixture, shape it into a 2-inch (5 cm) patty, and pack the mixture down so it won't fall apart. Place the patty on a plate or a tray. Repeat until you have used up all the tomato mixture.

Cover the bottom of a medium nonstick pan with olive oil at least ¼ inch (6 mm) deep, and bring to a frying temperature over medium heat. You can check the temperature of the oil by dipping the handle of a wooden spoon in it. When the oil is ready, it will gently sizzle and bubble up around the handle.

Line a plate with a paper towel.

Working in batches, fry 3 or 4 patties for 2 to 3 minutes on each side, until golden, using two forks to turn them. Take the patties

out and let them drain on the paper towel–lined plate. Repeat with the rest of the tomato patties, a third at a time.

Serve warm or at room temperature with tzatziki, if desired.

Leftover tomatokeftedes Santorinis can be stored in an airtight container in the refrigerator for up to 4 days. To reheat, warm in the oven at 325°F (160°C) for 6 to 8 minutes.

PHYLLO DOUGH

Phyllo means "leaf" in Greek, and the name refers to thin sheets of dough. Phyllo is categorized based on its ingredients and thickness. Some phyllo dough is made with just flour and water, while others include olive oil or butter.

When Greeks make phyllo sheets from scratch, they call it "opening the phyllo." This refers to the gradual thinning of the dough as it's rolled out with a rolling pin. In modern Greece, opening the phyllo is a mark of one's culinary skills. The finer the phyllo dough, the crunchier and lighter it will be when baked.

The most widely used phyllo dough in Greece is called phyllo kroustas; it's used for both savory and sweet pastries.

Here are some tips for working with phyllo:

- Thaw frozen dough gradually, at least 6 hours in the refrigerator.

- Prepare the filling ahead before working with the phyllo dough.

- Make sure your work surface is clean and dry. Always work in a cool environment and away from the heat of the oven or stove; otherwise, the phyllo will dry out too quickly.

- Cover the sheets that you're not using with a slightly damp kitchen towel to prevent them from drying out.

- Cut the sheets to the proper shape and size for the recipe before you begin working with them.

- Because phyllo dough is free of or low in fat, it needs to be brushed with oil or melted butter to prevent the sheets from sticking to one another or crumbling. Have olive oil or melted butter ready in a bowl, and brush only the sheets that you're working with.

- If the phyllo sheets tear or have holes, use a little oil or butter and patch them up with leftover dough.

Potato Pastry Rolls

PATATOPITAKIA

Makes 24 small pies

3 tablespoons extra-virgin olive oil

1 medium onion, finely chopped

4 medium Yukon Gold or russet potatoes, peeled, quartered, boiled, and mashed

Kosher salt and freshly ground black pepper to taste

26 ounces (750 g) puff pastry, thawed overnight in the refrigerator if frozen

1 medium egg

⅓ cup (40 g) sesame seeds

To serve
Tomato sauce (page 83; optional)

Potato pies are a great use for leftover mashed potatoes, with the addition of sautéed onions to pump up their flavor. These pies are perfect for lunch at work, picnics, or a kid's school lunch. Premade puff pastry makes this recipe quick and easy. I like to leave the edges unsealed so the filling can spill out a little and get crispy and golden in the oven.

Line two baking sheets with parchment paper.

In a small nonstick pan, heat the olive oil over medium heat. Add the onion and cook for 5 to 6 minutes, stirring occasionally, until the onion is soft and fragrant.

Transfer the cooked onion with the oil to a medium bowl. Add the mashed potatoes, salt, and pepper, and mix. Taste and adjust the seasoning, if needed.

On a clean work surface, unroll the puff pastry. Cut into 24 rectangles, 2½ by 3 inches (6.5 by 8 cm) each. Place a heaping teaspoon of the potato filling at the bottom of the short end of one rectangle, and roll it up like a cigar. Leave the ends unsealed, so the filling can peek out during the baking and turn crisp and golden where it is exposed. Repeat with the rest of the rectangles.

Arrange the rolls on the prepared baking sheets, 2 inches (5 cm) apart, seam-side down.

Whisk the egg with 1 teaspoon water in a small bowl. Brush the pies with the egg wash and sprinkle with the sesame seeds.

Preheat the oven to 350°F (175°C).

Transfer the baking sheets to the refrigerator for 15 to 20 minutes before baking.

Bake one pan at a time for 25 to 30 minutes, until the rolls are golden brown.

Serve warm or at room temperature, with tomato sauce, if desired.

(recipe continues)

Leftover patatopitakia can be stored in an airtight container in the refrigerator for up to 4 days. To reheat, warm in the oven at 325°F (160°C) for 6 to 8 minutes.

PUFF PASTRY DOUGH The Greeks
call puff pastry *sfoliata*, and it is the second most widely used type of dough in the country. Puff pastry is often credited as a French invention, but its origins are actually debated, with claims that it came from Egypt, Rome, or Greece. The first mention of puff pastry appears in a Spanish cookbook from the early seventeenth century, and the original version was made with flour and oil and often filled with fruits and nuts. Since then, it has evolved into the pastry dough we know today, which is made with cooled fat (usually butter) folded many times into the dough to create discrete alternating layers of fat and dough. Puff pastry is thicker than phyllo dough and is easier and faster to work with. It creates a softer and richer wrap for the filling, but the result won't be as crispy as phyllo dough.

To thaw frozen puff pastry dough, defrost it in the refrigerator for at least 8 hours. It will keep, covered, in the refrigerator for up to 3 days. Don't freeze the dough again after it has been thawed.

It's best to work with puff pastry dough straight from the refrigerator, while it's still cold. If it warms up while you're working with it, return it to the refrigerator for a 30-minute burst of cold air, and then try again.

Once formed, puff pastry should rest in the refrigerator or freezer for a few minutes before baking. The transition from cold to hot will make the pastries airier and crispier.

Spinach Pie

SPANAKOPITA

Makes one 9-by-13-inch (23 by 33 cm) rectangular pie or one 12-inch (30 cm) round pie

⅔ cup (160 ml) plus ¼ cup (60 ml) extra-virgin olive oil

1 medium onion, finely chopped

1 medium leek, finely chopped

1⅓ pounds (600 g) fresh spinach, well rinsed and coarsely chopped

14 ounces (400 g) feta, coarsely crumbled

7 ounces (200 g) ricotta

3 or 4 scallions (white and light green parts only), thinly sliced

1 cup (30 g) finely chopped fresh dill

2 large eggs

½ teaspoon kosher salt

½ teaspoon freshly ground black pepper

¼ teaspoon freshly ground nutmeg

3 tablespoons bread crumbs

14 sheets phyllo dough, thawed overnight in the refrigerator if frozen

The idea for spanakopita came from Byzantine pies filled with various boiled greens from the Greek countryside. Today there are many variations of spanakopita, depending on the filling, type of phyllo dough, method of preparation, and region of origin. No matter how it's made, this pie is a popular snack for people on the go, as well as a hearty main dish for sit-down dinners. Spinach pies are enjoyed year-round, and in many parts of Greece, they're a staple of Christmas and New Year's celebrations.

This iconic Greek staple was originally vegan, with a filling of sautéed spinach, onion, and herbs. Today feta and eggs are often added, and another welcome addition is ricotta, which gives the dish an extra creaminess. If you want to try the vegan version, you can leave out the eggs and cheeses.

In a large nonstick pan, heat ¼ cup (60 ml) of the olive oil over medium heat. Add the onion and leek and cook for 8 to 10 minutes, stirring occasionally, until the onion and leek are soft and fragrant.

Transfer the cooked onion and leek to a large bowl.

Add the spinach to the same pan (no need to add oil) and sauté for 3 to 4 minutes over medium heat, stirring occasionally, until the spinach is wilted and loses its volume. Transfer the cooked spinach to a colander and cool completely.

Squeeze the water from the cooked spinach with your hands, working one handful at a time, and add the spinach to the bowl with the onion. Add the feta, ricotta, scallions, dill, eggs, salt, pepper, and nutmeg, and mix.

Preheat the oven to 350°F (175°C).

Sprinkle the bread crumbs evenly on the bottom of a 9-by-13-inch (23 by 33 cm) glass or metal baking pan or a 12-inch (30 cm) round baking pan.

On a clean work surface, unroll the phyllo sheets and cover them with a slightly damp kitchen towel.

(recipe continues)

Lay 2 phyllo sheets on the bottom of the pan, letting the edges hang over the sides of the pan, and brush with a little of the remaining olive oil. Place a phyllo sheet half in the pan and half hanging outside it. Repeat on the other three sides of the pan so that the 4 sheets overlap in the middle, and brush with a little olive oil. Lay 2 more sheets in the center of the pan for 8 layers of phyllo sheets in total. Spread the spinach filling evenly inside the pan.

Fold all the phyllo sheets hanging outside the pan over the filling; they should overlap completely. Brush with a little olive oil. Crinkle each of the 6 remaining phyllo sheets like an accordion and lay them on top, one next to the other, to create a wrinkled cover pattern. Brush with a little olive oil.

Before baking, use a large knife to cut through the top layers of the spanakopita just until you reach the filling. If using a rectangular pan, cut into 15 to 20 squares; if using a round pan, cut into 8 to 16 wedges. Precutting makes the pie much easier to serve, as phyllo dough becomes crisp and crumbly after baking.

Bake uncovered for 50 to 60 minutes, until the pie is golden brown. Let rest for 10 minutes before cutting and serving.

Leftover spanakopita can be stored covered in the refrigerator for up to 4 days. To reheat, warm in the oven at 325°F (160°C) for 10 to 15 minutes.

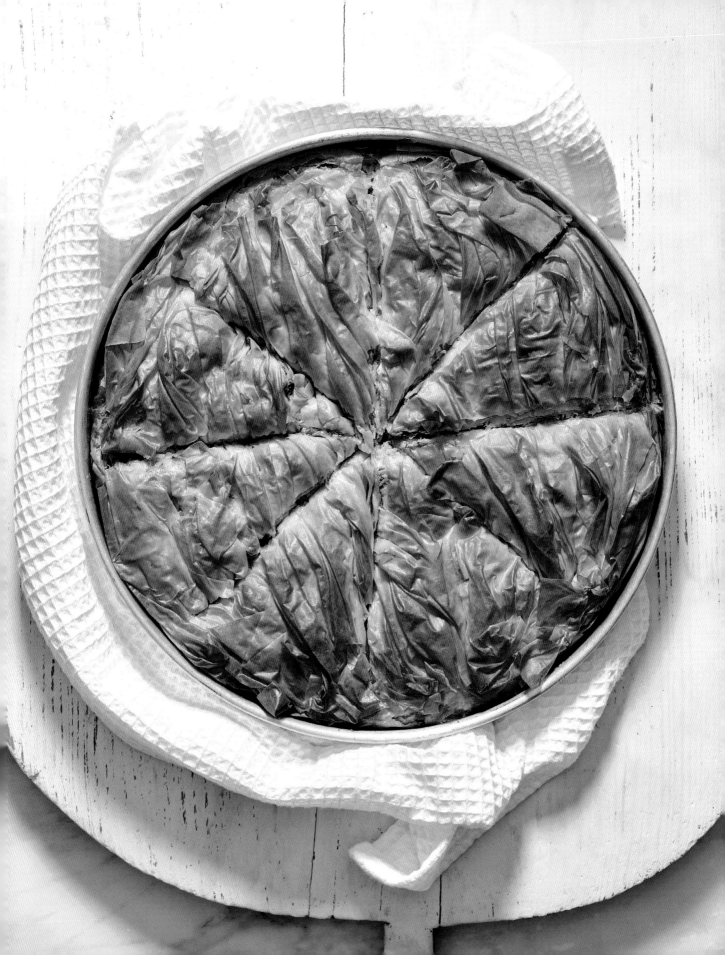

Cheese Pie

TIROPITA

Serves 8 to 12

13 ounces (370 g) feta, coarsely crumbled

7 ounces (200 g) ricotta

½ cup (50 g) finely grated Parmesan

⅓ cup (10 g) finely chopped fresh dill

2 tablespoons finely chopped fresh mint

2 large eggs

½ teaspoon kosher salt

½ teaspoon freshly ground black pepper

¼ teaspoon freshly ground nutmeg

12 sheets phyllo dough, thawed overnight in the refrigerator if frozen

⅓ cup (80 ml) extra-virgin olive oil

Pies in Greece are like pizza in Italy, and tiropita is the undisputed queen of Greek pies. It is sold in every bakery, and many cafés offer a breakfast special that includes coffee and tiropita. Although it's a popular street food, it's also a dish people prepare at home. A large tray feeds the whole family. While there are many versions, the traditional variety is filled with feta and eggs. The rest of the ingredients in the filling are left up to the personal preference of whoever is preparing the pastry. Of course, the quality of the cheeses is critical and will determine the flavor. I like a filling that contains the holy trinity of feta, ricotta, and Parmesan. The pastry is finished in a beautiful spiral shape.

Preheat the oven to 350°F (175°C). Line a baking sheet with parchment paper.

In a large bowl, combine the feta, ricotta, Parmesan, dill, mint, eggs, salt, pepper, and nutmeg.

On a clean work surface, unroll the phyllo sheets and cover them with a slightly damp kitchen towel.

Stack 2 phyllo sheets and brush the top with a little olive oil.

On the long side of the phyllo sheets, place a line of about one-sixth of the cheese filling and roll into a sausage shape. Coil the sausage into a spiral shape and place it in the center of the prepared baking sheet. Repeat with 2 more phyllo sheets and one-sixth more of the cheese stuffing. This time place the end of the sausage at the end of the first spiral in the pan to extend the shape. Repeat with the rest of the phyllo sheets and the filling, creating a large snail-shaped phyllo coil.

Brush the phyllo snail with a little olive oil.

Bake uncovered for 40 to 50 minutes, until the pie is golden brown. Let rest for 10 minutes before cutting and serving.

Leftover tiropita can be stored covered in the refrigerator for up to 4 days. To reheat, warm in the oven at 325°F (160°C) for 10 to 15 minutes.

Leek Pie

PRASSOPITA

Makes one 9-by-13-inch (23 by 33 cm) rectangular pie or one 12-inch (30 cm) round pie

⅔ cup (160 ml) plus ¼ cup (60 ml) extra-virgin olive oil

4 medium leeks, coarsely chopped

14 ounces (400 g) feta, coarsely crumbled

7 ounces (200 g) ricotta

3 or 4 scallions (white and light green parts only), thinly sliced

3 large eggs

1 teaspoon freshly ground black pepper

½ teaspoon kosher salt

3 tablespoons bread crumbs

14 sheets phyllo dough, thawed overnight in the refrigerator if frozen

The Greeks have used leeks in their cooking since ancient times; in fact, leek pies predate spinach pies by many centuries. The key to making the filling is to slowly sauté the leeks in olive oil until they caramelize and develop a rich flavor. Then add a generous amount of salty feta and ricotta for creaminess and eggs to bind everything together. The caramelized leeks lend a sweet and savory flavor profile that sets this dish apart from other green pies such as Spanakopita (page 97).

In a large nonstick pan, heat ¼ cup (60 ml) of the olive oil over medium heat. Add the leeks and cook for 10 to 15 minutes, stirring occasionally, until the leeks are soft and caramelized.

Transfer the leeks to a large bowl and cool completely.

Add the feta, ricotta, scallions, eggs, pepper, and salt, and mix.

Preheat the oven to 350°F (175°C).

Sprinkle the bread crumbs evenly on the bottom of a 9-by-13-inch (23 by 33 cm) glass or metal baking pan or a 12-inch (30 cm) round baking pan.

On a clean work surface, unroll the phyllo sheets and cover them with a slightly damp kitchen towel.

Lay 2 phyllo sheets on the bottom of the pan, letting the edges hang over the sides of the pan, and brush with a little of the remaining olive oil. Place a phyllo sheet half in the pan and half hanging outside it. Repeat on the other three sides of the pan so that the 4 sheets overlap in the middle, and brush with a little olive oil. Lay 2 more sheets in the center of the pan for 8 layers of phyllo sheets in total. Spread the leek filling evenly inside the pan.

Fold all the phyllo sheets hanging outside the pan over the filling and brush with a little olive oil. Cover with 2 phyllo sheets and brush with a little olive oil. Cover with 4 more phyllo sheets and brush with olive oil. Tuck in the excess dough from the sides.

Before baking, use a large knife to cut through the top layers of the prassopita just until you reach the filling. If using a rectangular pan,

cut into 15 to 20 squares; if using a round pan, cut into 8 to 16 wedges. Precutting makes it much easier to serve the pie, as phyllo dough becomes crisp and crumbly after baking.

Bake uncovered for 50 to 60 minutes, until the pie is golden brown. Let rest for 10 minutes before cutting and serving.

Leftover prassopita can be stored covered in the refrigerator for up to 4 days. To reheat, warm in the oven at 325°F (160°C) for 10 to 15 minutes.

Zucchini Pie

KOLOKITHOPITA

Serves 8 to 12

1 tablespoon extra-virgin olive oil

⅓ cup (35 g) plus 2 tablespoons bread crumbs

6 medium zucchini

7½ ounces (215 g) graviera or Gruyère, coarsely grated (about 3 packed cups)

7 ounces (200 g) ricotta

7 ounces (200 g) feta, coarsely crumbled

4 large eggs

1 teaspoon kosher salt

½ teaspoon freshly ground black pepper

Some would object to the name of this dish because there is no dough and therefore the suffix *pita*, meaning "pie," is inaccurate. Yet the region of Epirus in western Greece is famed for its delicious traditional doughless zucchini pie. Similar to a casserole, it is a great light alternative to the heavier dough-wrapped pies, plus it can be gluten-free if you use gluten-free bread crumbs. Just combine all the ingredients in a bowl, spread the mixture in a pan, sprinkle on some grated graviera or Gruyère, and bake it in the oven. Easy-peasy.

Preheat the oven to 350°F (175°C). Brush an 8-by-12-inch (20 by 30 cm) glass or ceramic baking dish with the olive oil. Sprinkle 2 tablespoons of the bread crumbs evenly on the bottom of the baking dish.

Trim the ends of the zucchini. Using the large holes of a box grater, grate the zucchini (be careful of your fingertips!).

Squeeze the water from the grated zucchini with your hands, working one handful at a time, or place all the grated zucchini in a cheesecloth bag and wring out the liquid. Transfer the zucchini to a large bowl. Add the remaining ⅓ cup (35 g) bread crumbs, 5 ounces (140 g/2 cups) of the graviera, the ricotta, feta, eggs, salt, and pepper, and stir.

Spread the zucchini mixture evenly inside the pan and smooth the top. Sprinkle the remaining 2½ ounces (75 g/1 cup) graviera on top.

Bake uncovered for 35 to 40 minutes, until the pie is golden brown. Let rest for 10 minutes before cutting and serving.

Leftover kolokithopita can be stored covered in the refrigerator for up to 4 days. To reheat, warm in the oven at 325°F (160°C) for 10 to 15 minutes.

Greek Flatbread

KASSIOPITA

Serves 6 to 8

¼ cup (60 ml) extra-virgin olive oil

2 large eggs

1 cup (240 ml) whole milk

1 cup (240 g) full-fat Greek yogurt

2 cups (250 g) all-purpose flour

½ teaspoon dried oregano

½ teaspoon kosher salt

½ teaspoon freshly ground black pepper

8 ounces (230 g) feta, coarsely crumbled (about 1½ cups)

2 tablespoons white or black sesame seeds (or both)

Kassiopita is another famous delicacy from the region of Epirus in western Greece. The simple flatbread contains ingredients you probably already have in your pantry, and it takes less than five minutes to make. No yeast or kneading is required—just combine all the ingredients in a bowl, pour the mixture into a baking dish, and sprinkle on the toppings. Great to eat alone or with spreads, it's also wonderful for sopping up all the delicious Greek salad juice. Preheating the oiled pan in the oven before baking produces a brown, crispy crust on the bottom and edges of the bread.

Preheat the oven to 350°F (175°C). Pour the olive oil into an 8-by-12-inch (20 by 30 cm) glass or ceramic baking dish so the oil covers the pan evenly.

Place the pan in the oven for 15 minutes, until the oil and the pan are very hot.

Meanwhile, in a large bowl, whisk the eggs. Add the milk and yogurt and whisk to combine.

Add the flour, oregano, salt, and pepper, and whisk until the batter is smooth and thick like pancake batter. Add 4 ounces (115 g/¾ cup) of the feta and mix with a spoon.

Remove the hot baking dish from the oven. Carefully pour the batter evenly into the hot pan and smooth the top. It's fine if some of the oil that was at the bottom of the pan pools over the top of the batter.

Sprinkle the remaining 4 ounces (115 g/¾ cup) feta and the sesame seeds on top.

Bake uncovered for 30 to 35 minutes, until the bread is golden brown on top and crispy on the edges. Let rest for 10 minutes before cutting and serving.

Leftover kassiopita can be stored covered in the refrigerator for up to 4 days. To reheat, warm in the oven at 325°F (160°C) for 6 to 8 minutes.

Thessaloniki Pretzels

KOULOURI THESSALONIKIS

Makes 6 pretzels

1⅓ cups (320 ml) lukewarm water

2 teaspoons (7 g) active dry yeast

3 tablespoons sugar

4 cups (500 g) all-purpose flour

3 tablespoons extra-virgin olive oil

1 teaspoon kosher salt

1½ cups (180 g) sesame seeds

These delicious bread rings, dotted with sesame seeds, crispy on the outside and soft on the inside, originated in Thessaloniki, Greece, in medieval times. They became popular throughout the Byzantine and Ottoman Empires, and today koulouri pretzels (also known as Thessaloniki bagels) are a favorite Greek breakfast on the go. Children take them to school, and adults eat them with coffee in the morning. If you've walked the streets of Athens or Thessaloniki, you've definitely come across the yellow food stalls selling them.

There are many variations of koulouri, with yeast and without, with eggs and egg-free. This vegan version goes well served with olive oil, savory spreads such as Tzatziki (page 25) and Fava (page 26), or sweet ones like jam and honey.

In the bowl of a stand mixer, use a spoon to mix the water, yeast, and sugar until the yeast and sugar dissolve completely. Let sit for 10 minutes, until the mixture is bubbly.

Attach the bowl to the mixer stand fitted with the dough hook. Add the flour, 2 tablespoons of the olive oil, and the salt, and mix on low speed for 6 to 8 minutes, until the dough is smooth and pulls away from the bowl.

Brush a clean large bowl with the remaining 1 tablespoon olive oil and place the dough inside. Cover the bowl with plastic wrap and let rest at room temperature for about 1 hour, until the dough doubles in size.

Preheat the oven to 400°F (200°C). Line three baking sheets with parchment paper.

Fill a wide bowl with water. Spread the sesame seeds on a large plate.

On a clean work surface, cut the dough into 6 even pieces, weighing about 5 ounces (135 grams) each.

Roll each piece into a rope about 24 inches (60 cm) long, bring the ends together to create a ring, and pinch them to secure. If the dough resists rolling, let it rest for 5 minutes, until it is more elastic.

(recipe continues)

Working one at a time, dip each ring in the water for 1 second and then into the sesame seeds so that the ring is covered well with seeds.

Place 2 sesame rings on each baking sheet. Reshape them on the pan if they have lost their ring form. Let rest at room temperature for 15 to 20 minutes, until the rings rise a little.

Bake one sheet at a time for 15 to 20 minutes (give priority to the pan with the pretzels that you shaped first), until the pretzels are golden and crusty.

Serve warm or at room temperature.

Leftover koulouri Thessalonikis can be stored covered at room temperature for up to 3 days. To reheat, warm in the oven at 325°F (160°C) for 6 to 8 minutes.

THE PATH
OF THE OLIVE

Greece is a country bathed in sunlight and shaded by olive trees. The history of the olive tree has been intertwined with that of Greece and its people for thousands of years. The olive has made its way into all corners of Greek life. Passed down from generation to generation, olive trees are prized assets, often presented as wedding gifts to newlyweds by their parents.

Defying strong winds, able to grow in a variety of soils, needing little water, and with deep roots, the olive tree is hardy and long-lived. Growing olives and producing olive oil were common eight thousand years ago in the area where Syria, Lebanon, Israel, and West Jordan are located today. In prehistoric times, people in the Greek peninsula began cultivating olive trees by domesticating wild varieties of olives that grew in the eastern Mediterranean. The tree begins to bear fruit when it is between seven and fifteen years old and will reach full maturity between the third and seventh decades of its life. Olive trees bloom between April and May, and their pollen is dispersed by the wind. By the end of October, the fruit is fully ripe. Harvesting the olives begins in November and lasts in some areas until March. With proper care, an olive tree can live for thousands of years. Crete boasts the oldest living olive tree in the world, estimated to be between two and four thousand years old.

Even in ancient times, Greek olive oil was famed for its superior quality and was in great demand throughout the known world. The ancient Greek cities prospered through the marine trade of olive oil, which made Athens one of the wealthiest cities in the Mediterranean. According to Greek mythology, the gods and demigods gifted humankind with the olive. Apollo sent his son Aristaeus to teach Greeks how to cultivate the olive tree, and it was mighty Hercules who decreed that the winners of the Olympic games be crowned with a wreath made from olive branches. Athena, the goddess of wisdom, taught the ancient Athenians the secrets of the olive. To express their gratitude to the goddess for introducing them to this magical fruit that brought them riches, healed wounds, and provided sustenance as well as adding aroma and flavor to their lives, the Greek people named their city after the goddess. The olive has even been incorporated into modern religious practices. In Greek Orthodoxy, olive trees are associated with the hope of resurrection and eternal life, and olive oil is used in ceremonies such as baptisms, weddings, and memorials.

Whole communities participate in the olive harvest, with even children helping to collect the olives before the winter rainy season. Today, wherever olive trees grow, harvesttime is marked by the smell of freshly squeezed olive oil produced by the local mills.

Olives and olive oil, aka "liquid gold," are staples in Greek cuisine and are used in almost every meal. Olives are eaten raw as a delicacy all day and served with each meal, and are incorporated into many dishes, such as Baked Feta (page 55) and Meatballs in Tomato Sauce with Olives (page 201). Most Greek foods are cooked with extra-virgin olive oil, and the rich, fresh oil is drizzled over salads and cold and warm dishes, such as Greek Salad (page 39), Dakos (page 34), and Horta (page 173). Today Greece consumes more olive oil per capita than any other nation in the world—a staggering average of more than 24 liters per person per year. Greeks are proud of the history and quality of their olives and olive oil. And Greece is home to many local, regional, national, and international competitions centered around olives; a win or even an honorable mention in one of these contests brings status and prestige not only to individual growers and producers but also to the regions where their olives originate. Perhaps the best summary of the influence of the olive on Greek culture was given to us by the Greek poet Odysseas Elytis, who was awarded the Nobel Prize in Literature in 1979. As Elytis put it:

If you deconstruct Greece,
In the end you will be left with
an olive tree, a vineyard, and a boat.

THREE

STUFFED VEGETABLES

Greek cuisine is centered around fresh and seasonal vegetables. Even in ancient Greece, vegetables were in high demand—and not just for Pythagoras's followers, who were conscientious vegetarians. In cities and villages, the daily menu included artichokes, beets, aromatics, cucumbers, cabbages, lettuces, pumpkins, turnips, and mushrooms. Many used vegetables for medicinal purposes. With the advent of Christianity and its prohibition against eating meat during holy days, vegetables became even more important in the Greek diet, and stuffing vegetables with grains and cheeses turned out to be an excellent way to get a satisfying meal out of them. Stuffed vegetables are most often served as the main course of a meal—in many parts of the country, with thick Greek yogurt and a cup of retsina or ouzo on the side.

Stuffed vegetables are incredibly versatile. The fillings can be customized to fit any diet or flavor preference—vegan, vegetarian, loaded with meat—and cooked in sauces that range from rich to mild. Preparing stuffed vegetables is not a quick process, but it isn't complicated or difficult, either. It requires only some time and patience. What's certain is that the investment pays off, because there is nothing like a warm pot or pan of stuffed zucchini, peppers, or tomatoes to create a soul-satisfying meal.

When preparing a rice-based filling, it's best to use a round or short-grain rice, like arborio or carnaroli. This type of rice will soften during cooking but hold its shape, unifying the filling ingredients. Before stuffing the vegetables, taste the filling and make sure it is well seasoned. Err on the side of a little extra salt, because the vegetable vessels will absorb some of it during the cooking or baking process. Always let vegetables stuffed with rice rest for at least 15 minutes before serving: The juices will redistribute, the flavors will blend, and the stuffed vegetables will firm up and stay moist. These stuffed vegetables taste even better the next day. The extra time allows all the flavors to deepen. To reheat stuffed vegetables that have been refrigerated, take them out of the refrigerator 45 to 60 minutes early so that they reach room temperature. Then cover with aluminum foil and heat in the oven for 15 to 20 minutes at 325°F (160°C).

Stuffed Grape Leaves

DOLMADES

Makes about 36 dolmades

One 12-ounce (340 g drained) jar
grape leaves (at least 50 leaves
in case some tear) or 50 fresh or
frozen grape leaves

5 tablespoons extra-virgin
olive oil

¼ cup (35 g) pine nuts

¾ cup (135 g) uncooked short-
grain rice, preferably arborio
or carnaroli

1 small zucchini

3 tablespoons tomato paste

1 tablespoon lemon zest

5 tablespoons lemon juice

1 or 2 scallions (white and light
green parts only), thinly sliced

⅓ cup (8 g) finely chopped
fresh flat-leaf parsley

⅓ cup (10 g) finely chopped
fresh dill

⅓ cup (7 g) finely chopped
fresh mint

1½ teaspoons kosher salt

1 teaspoon freshly ground
black pepper

2 cups (480 ml) warm water

To serve
Tzatziki (page 25; optional)

The famous Greek dolmades are so adored that the dish has its own patron saint: Saint John the Theologian. The Greek Orthodox Church honors this saint every December 27, and in Crete, the devout gather in churches to have their dolmades blessed by the saint before sharing them with family and friends.

Dolmades can be enjoyed either cold or at room temperature, as a snack or an appetizer, and they make a wonderful addition to picnics or party buffets. There are many variations to this recipe. The secret here is the addition of grated zucchini to the filling, which makes the dolmades juicier and more flavorful. If you are lucky enough to find fresh grape leaves in your local market or perhaps in your garden, use them. For the rest of us, canned vine leaves will do the job. The younger the leaf, the tastier and less fibrous it will be, but younger leaves will also be smaller, thinner, and more delicate, and therefore a little more difficult to work with.

If you are using grape leaves from a jar, rinse them under cold water to get rid of the salt. Drain well. If you are using fresh or frozen grape leaves, see the sidebar on grape leaves (page 125). Trim off and discard any tough stems from the base of each leaf.

Line the bottom of a 10-inch (25 cm) pot with 7 or 8 grape leaves. You can use torn leaves for the bottom of the pot—save the nice whole leaves for the filling.

Heat a small pan over medium heat. Add 3 tablespoons of the olive oil and the pine nuts and toast the pine nuts, stirring occasionally, for 2 to 3 minutes, until golden. Transfer the pine nuts with the olive oil to a medium bowl.

Rinse the rice in a fine-mesh sieve under cold water until the water runs clear, and drain. Transfer the rice to the bowl with the pine nuts.

Trim the ends of the zucchini. Using the large holes of a box grater, grate the zucchini (be careful of your fingertips!). Squeeze the water from the grated zucchini with your hands, working one handful at a time, or place all the grated zucchini in a cheesecloth bag and wring out the liquid. Transfer the zucchini to the bowl with the rice.

(recipe continues)

Add the tomato paste, lemon zest, 3 tablespoons of the lemon juice, the scallions, parsley, dill, mint, 1 teaspoon of the salt, and ½ teaspoon of the pepper to the bowl, and mix.

On a clean work surface, arrange a grape leaf with the glossy side down and the side with the veins up. Place 1 heaping teaspoon of the rice filling in the lower third of the leaf. Fold the bottom over the filling, then fold the sides over the filling and roll, tucking in the left and right sides as you roll up to cover the filling. (The action is similar to rolling spring rolls or burritos.) If the leaf tears while you're working, remove the filling and place it on another whole leaf. Do not overload the leaf with too much filling. A teaspoon is sufficient, leaving room for the rice to absorb the liquid and swell. Repeat with the remaining leaves.

Arrange the stuffed grape leaves in a single layer in the pot, seam-side down. Pack them in snugly together in a circular pattern from the outside of the pot to the center.

In a small jar or pitcher, combine the water with the remaining 2 tablespoons olive oil, 2 tablespoons lemon juice, ½ teaspoon salt, and ½ teaspoon pepper. Pour the mixture over the stuffed grape leaves. Carefully place an inverted plate on top of the dolmades to keep them from floating.

Bring the liquid to a boil over high heat, reduce the heat to a simmer, cover the pot, and simmer for 60 minutes, until all the water is absorbed. Turn off the heat and use tongs to remove the plate from the pot. Let the dolmades rest for 10 minutes and serve warm, at room temperature, or cold with tzatziki, if desired.

Leftover dolmades can be stored in an airtight container in the refrigerator for up to 5 days.

GRAPE LEAVES
In Greece, grapevine leaves are stuffed with rice, cheese, or minced meat. They are also used to wrap grilled fish or chunks of meat. If you are lucky enough to have access to fresh grape leaves, use them to make dolmades.

Choose light-colored medium-sized soft grape leaves, ones without holes. It's best to pick the leaves toward the end of spring, when they are still fresh. During the summer, the leaves will be hard and too thick and chewy due to exposure to the sun.

After you pick the leaves, you can freeze them unwashed in plastic zip-lock bags or airtight containers. Freezing and thawing the leaves will soften them anyway, so there is no need to cook them before using. Thaw the leaves, wash them well, and they are ready to go.

If you are using freshly picked leaves, blanch them in a pot with boiling water and a tablespoon of salt for 50 to 60 seconds, until their color changes from light green to a muted dark green, almost khaki.

If you are using leaves from a jar, make sure to wash off the salt used as a preservative solution. Rinse the leaves for 2 minutes under cold water and drain well. Store-bought leaves do not need to be blanched; they are ready for filling.

Stuffed Tomatoes

DOMATES GEMISTES

Makes 10 stuffed tomatoes

10 large tomatoes

¼ cup (60 ml) plus 3 tablespoons extra-virgin olive oil

2 medium onions, finely chopped

1 teaspoon dried oregano

Kosher salt and freshly ground black pepper to taste

1 cup (180 g) uncooked short-grain rice, preferably arborio or carnaroli

⅓ cup (45 g) pine nuts

1¾ cups (420 ml) warm water

¼ to ½ teaspoon dried chili flakes (optional)

½ cup (12 g) finely chopped fresh flat-leaf parsley

½ cup (15 g) finely chopped fresh dill

¼ cup (5 g) finely chopped fresh mint

To serve

Tzatziki (page 25; optional)

Tomatoes were first grown in Greece in the early 1800s by a group of Capuchin monks in a monastery in Athens. Although at first tomatoes were used in desserts, today they are a staple of Greek cuisine and are a perfect vegetable for filling. Choose ripe but firm tomatoes that are about the same size, so they will cook evenly. To minimize waste, the pulp that is removed from the tomatoes is used to make the sauce. This dish is also vegan and good for you.

Cut off the tops of the tomatoes and reserve them. Using a teaspoon, scoop out the insides of the tomatoes without breaking the outer skin, leaving a ¼-inch (6 mm) rim on all sides. Set the tomatoes aside.

Transfer the tomato pulp to a cutting board and coarsely chop it. Transfer the pulp and juice to a 9-by-13-inch (23 by 33 cm) glass, metal, or ceramic baking dish.

In a large nonstick pan, heat ¼ cup (60 ml) of the olive oil over medium heat. Add the onion and cook for 5 to 6 minutes, stirring occasionally, until the onion is soft and fragrant.

Transfer 1 heaping tablespoon of the cooked onion to the baking dish with the tomato pulp. Add the oregano, salt, and pepper to the pulp mixture and stir. Taste and adjust the seasoning, if needed.

Transfer the rest of the cooked onion to a small bowl and set aside.

Rinse the rice in a fine-mesh sieve under cold water until the water runs clear, and drain. In the same pan, heat 2 tablespoons olive oil over medium heat. Add the pine nuts and toast, stirring occasionally, for 2 to 3 minutes, until golden.

Add the rice to the same pan; there's no need to add oil. Add the reserved onion and cook over medium heat, stirring constantly, for 1 to 2 minutes, until the rice is coated in the oil, shiny and warm.

Add the water, salt, pepper, and chili flakes (if using), and mix. Bring to a boil over high heat. Reduce the heat to low and simmer uncovered for 6 to 8 minutes, until the water is absorbed into the rice and the rice is slightly undercooked.

Preheat the oven to 350°F (175°C).

Add the parsley, dill, and mint to the rice mixture and stir to combine. Taste and adjust the seasoning, if needed.

Stuff the reserved tomatoes with the rice filling, and cover each one with a tomato top.

Place the stuffed tomatoes in the baking dish on top of the sauce and drizzle with the remaining 1 tablespoon olive oil.

Bake uncovered for 40 to 45 minutes, until the tomatoes are golden brown. Let rest for 10 minutes and serve warm, with tzatziki, if desired.

Leftover domates gemistes can be stored in an airtight container in the refrigerator for up to 5 days. To reheat, warm in the oven at 325°F (160°C) for about 10 minutes.

PINE NUTS

Pine nuts are actually the edible seeds of several pine species. They have a nutty flavor with a little sweetness, and they are rich in vitamin E, iron, and magnesium. They boost energy, control blood glucose levels, and improve vision. If you find a bitter-tasting pine nut, it's a sign that the natural oils in them have turned rancid over time, and they are no longer good for use.

In Greek cuisine, pine nuts are essential ingredients in the filling for dolmades and other stuffed vegetables as well as in sweet and savory pastries. You can toast pine nuts in a pan without oil, but then they tend to brown unevenly, so it's best to add a little oil to the pan—and as a bonus, you can use this flavor-infused oil in the filling as well.

Stuffed Peppers with Cheese

PIPERIES GEMISTES

Makes 8 to 10 stuffed peppers

1 heaping tablespoon kosher salt, plus more to taste

8 to 10 long mild chili peppers, such as Romano, Anaheim, or poblano

5 ounces (140 g) feta, coarsely crumbled

3½ ounces (100 g) graviera or Gruyère, coarsely grated

½ cup (120 g) sour cream

3 tablespoons extra-virgin olive oil

2 or 3 garlic cloves, minced or grated

2 to 3 tablespoons finely chopped fresh flat-leaf parsley

Freshly ground black pepper to taste

This is a delicious low-carb summer dish that can be served as a first course or as a side. The peppers are poached in boiling water for a few minutes just to soften them a little before they are filled, while the rest of their cooking is done in the oven with the cheesy stuffing. You don't need to peel off the thin skin of the peppers, as you must in a roasted pepper salad. You can also play with the filling to make your own combination of flavors; check out the variations below.

Fill a large pot with water and season with the salt. Bring to a boil.

Add the chili peppers and cook for 5 to 6 minutes, until they begin to soften. The peppers will float, but they will steam anyway. Drain well and allow the peppers to rest until cool enough to handle.

Preheat the oven to 350°F (175°C). Line a roasting pan with aluminum foil and place a sheet of parchment paper on top.

Dry the peppers with a paper towel. Make a lengthwise incision along each pepper without cutting it fully in half, making a kind of pocket for filling. Remove and discard the seeds and membranes of the peppers. Dry the insides of the peppers with a paper towel so that the water does not dilute the filling.

In a medium bowl, combine the feta, graviera, sour cream, 1 tablespoon of the olive oil, the garlic, parsley, and black pepper. Taste and adjust the seasoning, if needed.

Using a teaspoon, stuff each pepper with about 2 tablespoons of the cheese filling. Place the stuffed peppers in the prepared roasting pan, open sides up. Drizzle the remaining 2 tablespoons olive oil over the top.

Bake uncovered for 30 to 40 minutes, until the cheese filling is golden. Serve warm.

Leftover piperies gemistes can be stored in an airtight container in the refrigerator for up to 4 days. To reheat, warm in the oven at 325°F (160°C) for about 10 minutes.

Variations

Add one or more to the filling:

- 10 to 12 Kalamata olives, pitted and cut into quarters

- 1 or 2 scallions (white and light green parts only), thinly sliced

- 1 tablespoon lemon zest

- ½ to 1 teaspoon dried chili flakes

Stuffed Zucchini

KOLOKITHAKIA GEMISTA

Makes 8 zucchini boats

1 heaping tablespoon kosher salt, plus more to taste

4 medium zucchini

8 ounces (225 g) feta, coarsely crumbled

3½ ounces (100 g) graviera or Gruyère, coarsely grated

3 tablespoons finely chopped fresh dill

Freshly ground black pepper to taste

2 large eggs

¾ cup (75 g) bread crumbs

¾ cup (180 ml) extra-virgin olive oil

To serve

Tzatziki (page 25; optional)

One of the classic summer dishes of Greece is zucchini and zucchini blossoms stuffed with cheese. While the season for the blossoms is very short and they tend to be hard to find, the vegetable itself is sold everywhere and all year round. Serve the stuffed zucchini warm as an appetizer with cold tzatziki.

Fill a large pot with water and season with the salt. Bring to a boil.

Add the whole zucchini and cook for 5 to 6 minutes, until they start to soften. Drain well and allow the zucchini to rest until cool enough to handle.

Dry the zucchini with a paper towel. Cut each zucchini in half lengthwise. Using a teaspoon, scoop out the center, leaving a ¼-inch (6 mm) rim on all sides of the vegetable to create boats. You can use the pulp to make stock or soup. Dry the insides of the zucchini boats with a paper towel so that any residual water does not dilute the filling.

In a medium bowl, combine the feta, graviera, dill, and pepper. Taste and adjust the seasoning, if needed.

Stuff the cheese filling into the hollowed-out zucchini and pack down the filling so that it doesn't fall out while the zucchini are being fried. Place them on a plate or tray.

Whisk the eggs in a shallow medium bowl. Place the bread crumbs in another shallow bowl.

Dip a zucchini in the egg, stuffed side down. Lift it out, let it drip for a second, and then dredge it in the bread crumbs, stuffed side down, making sure the zucchini is evenly coated. Return the breaded zucchini to the plate or tray and repeat with the remaining zucchini.

Cover the bottom of a medium nonstick pan with olive oil about ¼ inch (6 mm) deep, and bring to a frying temperature over medium heat. You can check the temperature of the oil by dipping the handle of a wooden spoon in it. When the oil is ready, it will gently sizzle and bubble up around the handle.

(recipe continues)

Line a plate with a paper towel.

Working in batches, fry 3 or 4 zucchini boats for 3 to 4 minutes, stuffed side down. Use tongs to turn them, and fry for 2 to 3 minutes on the other side. Take the fried zucchini out and let them drain on the paper towel-lined plate. Repeat with the remaining stuffed zucchini. Serve warm with tzatziki, if desired.

Leftover kolokithakia gemista can be stored in an airtight container in the refrigerator for up to 4 days. To reheat, warm in the oven at 325°F (160°C) for about 10 minutes.

Stuffed Vegetables

GEMISTA LAHANIKA

Makes 6 stuffed peppers and 6 stuffed tomatoes

6 medium bell peppers

6 large tomatoes

1 cup (180 g) uncooked short-grain rice, preferably arborio or carnaroli

½ cup (120 ml) extra-virgin olive oil

2 medium onions, finely chopped

5 or 6 garlic cloves, finely chopped

¾ pound (340 g) ground chuck

2½ cups (600 ml) warm water

3 tablespoons tomato paste

Kosher salt and freshly ground black pepper to taste

½ cup (12 g) finely chopped fresh flat-leaf parsley

½ cup (15 g) finely chopped fresh dill

⅓ cup (7 g) finely chopped fresh mint

This colorful dish is one of the most popular comfort foods in Greece. For many, it evokes childhood memories of summer. The most common version of this dish includes a vegetable combination of bell peppers, tomatoes, and round zucchini stuffed with rice and meat. This is an ideal recipe to make when you want a whole meal in one pan. *Gemista* means "stuffed," and boy, this is truly an excellent stuffing. The rice and meat are enriched by tomato paste, fresh herbs, and lots of sautéed onions and garlic, and absorb deep flavors from the tomatoes and peppers that hold the filling.

Cut off the tops of the bell peppers and reserve the tops. Remove and discard the seeds and membranes.

Cut off the tops of the tomatoes and reserve them. Using a teaspoon, scoop out the insides of the tomatoes without breaking the outer skin, leaving a ¼-inch (6 mm) rim on all sides. Set the tomatoes aside. Coarsely chop the tomato pulp and transfer it to a medium bowl. Set aside.

Rinse the rice in a fine-mesh sieve under cold water until the water runs clear, and drain.

In a large nonstick pan, heat ¼ cup (60 ml) of the olive oil over medium heat. Add the onions and garlic and cook for 5 to 6 minutes, stirring occasionally, until the onions and garlic are soft and fragrant.

Add the ground beef and cook, stirring and crumbling the beef, for 4 to 6 minutes, until the meat loses its pink color.

Add the rice, reserved tomato pulp, 1½ cups of the water, the tomato paste, salt, and black pepper to the pan with the beef, and stir to combine. Bring the mixture to a boil over high heat, reduce the heat to low, and simmer uncovered for 6 to 8 minutes, until the water is absorbed into the rice. The rice should be slightly undercooked.

Preheat the oven to 350°F (175°C).

(recipe continues)

Add the parsley, dill, and mint to the pan with the rice mixture, and stir to combine. Taste and adjust the seasoning, if needed.

Stuff the reserved peppers and tomatoes with the beef filling, and cover each one with a top.

Pour the remaining 1 cup water into a 9-by-13-inch (23 by 33 cm) glass, metal, or ceramic baking dish.

Place the stuffed peppers and tomatoes in the water and drizzle with the remaining 1/4 cup (60 ml) olive oil. Cover the dish with aluminum foil.

Bake covered for 60 minutes. Remove the aluminum foil and bake uncovered for another 40 to 45 minutes, until the stuffed vegetables are golden brown and bubbling. Let rest for 10 minutes and serve warm.

Leftover gemista lahanika can be stored in an airtight container in the refrigerator for up to 3 days. To reheat, warm in the oven at 325°F (160°C) for about 15 minutes.

Variation

It is very common in Greece to serve this dish with roasted potatoes for a more substantial meal.

Cut 4 peeled medium potatoes lengthwise into 6 long wedges each. In a medium bowl, toss the potatoes with 2 tablespoons olive oil, ½ teaspoon dried oregano, and salt and black pepper to taste. Scatter the potatoes in the pan between the stuffed vegetables, so that they bake at the same time. Serve the potatoes alongside the stuffed vegetables.

Stuffed Eggplant

PAPOUTSAKIA GEMISTA

Makes 6 stuffed eggplant halves

3 medium Italian or globe eggplants, skin on

6 tablespoons extra-virgin olive oil

Kosher salt and freshly ground black pepper to taste

1 medium onion, finely chopped

3 or 4 garlic cloves, finely chopped

1 pound (450 g) ground chuck

One 14-ounce (400 g) can crushed tomatoes

3 tablespoons finely chopped fresh flat-leaf parsley

2 tablespoons finely chopped fresh mint

4½ ounces (125 g) coarsely grated graviera or Gruyère

Papoutsakia means "little shoes" in Greek, a reference to the shape of this dish. Traditionally, the eggplants are first seasoned and baked until soft, then stuffed with a delicious ground meat and tomato sauce, topped with a béchamel, and baked again. Here is an easier, lighter, and faster version with grated cheese on top instead of béchamel sauce. If you want to stick to the classic way, you can find instructions for making béchamel in the recipe for Moussaka (page 211).

Preheat the oven to 350°F (175°C). Line a roasting pan with aluminum foil and place a sheet of parchment paper on top.

Cut the eggplants lengthwise. Score the flesh of each eggplant in a zigzag pattern so that the eggplants bake evenly. Drizzle with 3 tablespoons of the olive oil on the cut side, and season with salt and pepper. Place the eggplants in the prepared pan, cut-side down.

Bake uncovered for 40 to 50 minutes, until the eggplants are soft and their skin is golden brown.

Meanwhile, prepare the filling. In a large nonstick pan, heat the remaining 3 tablespoons olive oil over medium heat. Add the onion and garlic and cook for 5 to 6 minutes, stirring occasionally, until the onion and garlic are soft and fragrant.

Add the ground beef and cook, stirring and crumbling the meat, for 4 to 6 minutes, until the meat loses its pink color.

Add the crushed tomatoes and stir. Bring to a boil over high heat, reduce the heat to low, and simmer uncovered for 20 to 25 minutes, until most of the liquid has evaporated, leaving a thick sauce.

Add the parsley and mint and stir. Taste and adjust the seasoning, if needed.

When the eggplants have cooked, turn them over so that the cut side faces up. Mash the tops of the eggplants with the back of a spoon to make room for the filling. Divide the meat filling among the 6 eggplant halves. Sprinkle the graviera evenly over the tops.

Return the pan to the oven and bake for 15 to 20 minutes, until the cheese is golden. Serve immediately.

Leftover papoutsakia gemista can be stored in an airtight container in the refrigerator for up to 3 days. To reheat, warm in the oven at 325°F (160°C) for about 10 minutes.

Stuffed Cabbage

LAHANODOLMADES

Makes about 15 stuffed cabbage leaves

1 heaping tablespoon plus 1 teaspoon kosher salt

1 large green cabbage

1 medium onion, cut in quarters

1 handful fresh flat-leaf parsley

1 handful fresh dill

⅔ cup (120 g) uncooked short-grain rice, preferably arborio or carnaroli

⅔ pound (300 g) ground chuck

2 tablespoons extra-virgin olive oil

1 tablespoon lemon zest

½ to 1 teaspoon freshly ground black pepper

4 cups (960 ml) warm water

For the avgolemono

3 large eggs

2 tablespoons cornstarch

½ cup (120 ml) lemon juice

½ teaspoon kosher salt

If you enter a Greek house in winter and peek into the pots on the stove, one of them will likely contain stuffed cabbage, a dish that's a real classic with a long history. In ancient Athens, babies would be given cabbage leaves stuffed with meat to make them stronger, while in medieval times, boiled cabbage leaves stuffed with rice and raisins was a favorite dessert. In modern Greece, stuffed cabbage leaves are also prepared as a Christmas delicacy because of the association of the folding of the leaves with the wrapping of blankets around the newborn baby Jesus in the manger.

There are several ways to soften and prepare the cabbage leaves for filling. You can freeze the whole cabbage for at least twelve hours and then thaw it. You can cook the whole head in boiling water for a few minutes and then break it into leaves. Or you can break the head of cabbage into leaves when it's raw and then blanch a few leaves at a time. I find that the second method, cooking the whole head of cabbage at one time, is the easiest, but it is entirely up to you to decide. When the stuffed cabbage is cooked and ready, you add avgolemono, a velvety egg and lemon sauce. Greeks also use this tangy sauce in dishes with fish, meat, patties, or stuffed grape leaves, and even as a base for soups (see pages 158 and 161).

Fill a large pot two-thirds of the way with water and season with the 1 heaping tablespoon salt. Make sure the pot is not too full, because adding the cabbage raises the water level significantly. Bring the water to a boil.

With a sharp knife, carefully carve a circle around the core of the cabbage and remove it. Gently plunge the cabbage into the boiling water, cored-side down, and cook over medium-low heat for 6 minutes.

Use two large slotted spoons to turn the cabbage over, cored-side up, and cook for another 6 minutes, until the leaves separate from the cabbage easily. Carefully remove the cabbage from the water and place it in a colander. Reserve the pot with the water; if the inner leaves of the cabbage are still firm, you might need to boil them again so you can roll them up. Drain well and allow the cabbage to rest until cool enough to handle.

(recipe continues)

Place the onion, parsley, and dill in the bowl of a food processor and process to form a puree. Transfer the pureed vegetables to a medium bowl.

Rinse the rice in a fine-mesh sieve under cold water until the water runs clear, and drain. Transfer the rice to the bowl with the onion mixture. Add the ground beef, olive oil, lemon zest, the 1 teaspoon salt, and the pepper, and mix well.

Separate the cabbage leaves. If the inner leaves of the cabbage are too firm, put the cabbage back in the water and cook for another 2 to 3 minutes. Line the bottom of a 12-inch (30 cm) pot with 5 to 6 leaves. You can use torn leaves for the bottom of the pot; save the nice whole leaves for the filling.

To assemble the cabbage rolls, cut off and discard the thick bottom of each leaf so that the leaf will be more flexible and easier to roll.

On a clean work surface, arrange a cabbage leaf rib-side up. Place 1 tablespoon of the meat filling in the lower third of the leaf. Fold the bottom over the filling, then fold the sides over the filling and roll, continuing to tuck in the left and right sides as you roll to cover the filling. (The action is similar to rolling spring rolls or burritos.) Repeat with the rest of the leaves. If the inner leaves are too small for filling, you can overlap two leaves together for one stuffed cabbage roll.

Arrange the stuffed cabbage leaves in a single layer in the pot seam-side down. Pack them in snugly together in a circular pattern from the outside of the pot to the center.

Pour the water over the stuffed cabbage leaves. Carefully place an inverted plate on top of the lahanodolmades to keep them from floating. Bring to a boil over high heat, reduce the heat to a simmer, cover the pot, and cook for 60 minutes.

Prepare the avgolemono sauce: Turn off the heat and use tongs to remove the plate from the pot. Remove 1 cup (240 ml) of the cooking liquid from the pot and place it in a small bowl. Be careful not to disrupt the stuffed cabbages when removing the liquid.

Whisk the eggs in a medium bowl. Add the cornstarch and whisk well.

Add the lemon juice and the ½ teaspoon salt and whisk. To temper the eggs, add the hot cooking liquid to the egg mixture and stir immediately. Strain the sauce through a fine-mesh sieve to remove any lumps.

Pour the strained sauce over the stuffed cabbage leaves and shake the pot (don't stir) so that the sauce covers the cabbage evenly. Bring to a boil and immediately turn off the heat. Cover the pot with the lid and let rest for 10 minutes. Serve warm.

Leftover lahanodolmades can be stored in an airtight container in the refrigerator for up to 3 days. To reheat, add ½ cup warm water and warm in a pot placed over medium heat for about 10 minutes.

Variation

For a vegetarian version: Instead of ground beef, use 2 medium zucchini, coarsely grated with the water squeezed out, and 1 large egg.

DRINKS: WINE, OUZO, TSIPOURO, AND MORE

In antiquity, wine was a way for Greeks to reach the divine. Long before the advent of Christianity and communion wine, libations were offered at the altar as well as the dinner table. Today wines and distilled spirits such as ouzo, tsipouro, and retsina are an essential part of the Greek food experience. Spirits are often made with regional ingredients, and the traditions around their production and enjoyment unite the Greek world. Spirits are often made with regional ingredients, and the traditions around their production and enjoyment unite Greek communities. Before and during meals, Greeks gather around the table and lift their glasses just above eye level, offering the toast of *Yamas!*—to our health!— and then downing their drinks, marking the moment and the importance of good friends and good food in Greek culture.

WINE

Grape seeds dating as early as 4000 BCE have been found in northern Greece; these are similar to those of modern winemaking varietals. During the Bronze Age, wine cultivation expanded throughout the Greek world, and during the second millennium BCE, Greek merchants spread wine cultivation to areas around the Mediterranean. By the classical era, wine had become an indispensable part of everyday life. Since intoxication was frowned upon, wine was always diluted with water. In fact, the literal translation of the Greek word for wine, *krasi*, is "mixture." The only time most ancient Greeks consumed undiluted wine was as part of their breakfast by dipping bread in it, a practice called akraton that is still followed today in some islands and monasteries.

Wine was connected to Dionysus, the god of vitality, and Greeks loved drinking wine at festive events called symposia, a term that translates as "drinking together." Since as early as 475 BCE, some of the most prized wines came from the islands of Chios, Samos, Lesvos, and Thassos, where the world's first Protected Designation of Origin (PDO) was later established. Socrates and Plato philosophized on the art of wine appreciation, and Aristotle, who was proud of his vineyards in northern Greece, wrote extensively about viniculture. With the advent of Christianity, large-scale wine cultivation came to be organized around monasteries. In Greek Orthodoxy, wine is an essential part of the Holy Communion, as well as of the baptismal, wedding, and funeral rituals. A custom shared by most wine growers in the country is the celebration of Saint Tryphon, the protector of winemakers. On the first day of February, all agricultural activities stop and vineyards are sprinkled with holy water for good luck, followed by a great feast with food, wine, and music. In some locales, a small patch of the vineyard is left uncultivated as an offering to the saint for his benefaction.

Most Greek vineyards are small family operations growing native and indigenous grape varieties. There are over three hundred local wine varieties in Greece, and many are appreciated for their quality around the world. Some of the most famous Greek wines are Savatiano, a moderate-acidity white wine from Attica; Assyrtiko, a dry white wine from the island of Santorini that goes great with seafood; Agiorgitiko, a red wine with fruit and caramel notes from Nemea in northern Greece; and Moschato, a sweet or semisweet white or red honey wine from the island of Samos made with spices and dried fruits.

OUZO

Ouzo is the national alcoholic beverage of Greece. This licorice-flavored spirit made from leftover grape must is recognized as a PDO product of Greece. Ouzo is a drink meant to be shared, often at the beginning, middle, and end of meals—and of course, at times, without a meal at all. It is served every day, but also for special occasions, such as weddings, baptisms, and New Year's. Ouzo is also used to welcome guests to one's home and to make friends out of strangers. It can be found in any Greek taverna, but Greeks love ouzo so much that they have special establishments called ouzeri dedicated to serving it. Ouzo is never refrigerated; instead, it is served at room temperature, and cold water or ice is added slowly as it gradually releases all its aromas.

Ouzo has been around in some form since ancient times. Archaeological evidence for the distillation of ouzo dating back to 500 BCE has been found on the island of Crete. What separates ouzo from the anise-based alcoholic beverages of other Mediterranean countries is the triple distillation process, which is still done using traditional techniques in handmade copper vessels. Ouzo is made exclusively with native herbs, essential oils, and fennel, which give the spirit its fragrance and delicate taste. Ouzo distilled on the mainland is dry, with a clean, sharp flavor that pairs well with dairy-heavy foods, smoked and spiced meats, and sharp cheeses. Ouzo varieties from the islands tend to have richer flavor profiles and aromas that perfectly complement the seafood served on the coasts. At the ouzeri, Greeks enjoy the spirit with small plates of salty, spicy, and sour appetizers balanced

by the anise-dominated sweetness of the ouzo.

In some areas, ouzo is also used as an ingredient in cooking. The island of Lesvos (which boasts some of the most ancient and best ouzo varieties in the country) is known for its aromatic meatballs made with ouzo and cumin and its prawns cooked in ouzo sauce. Greeks use ouzo medicinally as well, since it is believed to lower blood pressure and to have mild antiseptic and pain-relieving properties, making it one of the oldest folk cures for toothache.

TSIPOURO

Tsipouro is a brandy invented in the fourteenth century by monks in the monasteries of Mount Athos, in northern Greece. Like ouzo, it is a robust distilled spirit made by the distilling of pomace, grape skins and juices left in the tank after wine is pressed. Some tsipouro has an anise flavor, like ouzo, though not all. Unlike ouzo, tsipouro is drunk without adding water or ice. It is traditionally served in short glasses with an accompaniment of nuts, dried fruit, cheeses, olives, seafood, or meats. Thessaly, Epirus, and Macedonia are the top tsipouro-producing regions in the country, along with the island of Crete, where a local variety without anise called tsikoudia is made. Greeks love to enjoy tsipouro at its own dedicated drinking establishment, called a tsipouradika. Tsipouro is recognized as a PDO product of Greece.

RETSINA

A white resin-based wine, retsina originated in antiquity from the practice of using pine resin to seal amphorae, the pots used to age wine. The pine resin kept the wine from spoiling and infused it with a unique aroma. Eventually the Romans invented the technique of barreling wine, eliminating the need to use pine resin as a sealant for porous clay vessels, but Greeks had developed a liking for the taste and continued to make the drink. Today retsina is produced all over Greece, with Attica, Boeotia, and Euboea being the top producing regions. The European Union has classified retsina as a PDO product of Greece.

FOUR

SOUPS AND SIDES

The soups and sides of the Greek table remain true to their heritage. These recipes go back many years, with only minor changes, if any. The ingredients are humble, the preparation is easy, and the results are healthy and satisfying. In this way, many soups and sides capture the beauty of the Mediterranean diet, which is a reflection of the way everyday people ate in ancient times. Their nutrition was based on lots of vegetables, legumes, olive oil, and fish (if they lived near the sea), and very little meat. Horta (page 173), a simple but delicious side of green leaves cooked in salt water and served with olive oil and lemon juice, demonstrates how Greeks highlight their fresh and seasonal vegetables. And there's Briam (page 170), a mind-bogglingly delicious summer casserole that represents the category of dishes known as ladera—vegetables cooked in a generous amount of high-quality olive oil.

The Greeks specialize in nourishing and filling stews rather than light broths. Here you'll find simple vegetarian soups made with aromatics, root vegetables, and lentils or beans. On the more sumptuous side are Meatball Soup (page 161) and Kotosoupa Avgolemono (page 158), a lemon chicken soup enriched with a velvety egg sauce.

Rice has a special place in Greek cuisine, but until the 1960s, it was considered a luxury. Even its role in stuffed vegetables is relatively new; corn was more commonly used. To stretch their rice, Greeks often mix it with vegetables in one dish (an influence of Ottoman cuisine), as opposed to serving both separately. Today, rice is often served as a side, as with Spanakorizo (page 165), a creamy rice colored with fresh greens, which is actually a result of Spanish influence. Another popular side is Pilafi me Lahanika (page 166), rice flavored with spices, herbs, and nuts. The word *pilaf* in the name indicates that this dish originated in Turkey, but the Greeks have come up with infinite variations on the theme.

153

LENTIL SOUP

FAKES SOUPA

154

BEAN SOUP

FASOLADA

157

TOMATO AND ORZO SOUP

MANESTRA

158

LEMON CHICKEN SOUP

KOTOSOUPA AVGOLEMONO

161

MEATBALL SOUP

YOUVARLAKIA AVGOLEMONO

165

SPINACH RICE

SPANAKORIZO

166

RICE WITH VEGETABLES

PILAFI ME LAHANIKA

169

OKRA IN TOMATO SAUCE

BAMIES LATHERES ME DOMATES

170

ROASTED VEGETABLES

BRIAM

173

BOILED WILD LEAFY GREENS

HORTA

Lentil Soup

FAKES SOUPA

Serves 6 to 8

2 cups (320 g) dried brown or green lentils

⅓ cup (80 ml) extra-virgin olive oil

1 large onion, finely chopped

2 medium carrots, cut into ¼-inch (6 mm) cubes

2 celery stalks, cut into ¼-inch (6 mm) cubes

3 tablespoons tomato paste

2 teaspoons dried oregano

½ to 1 teaspoon dried chili flakes (optional)

Kosher salt and freshly ground black pepper to taste

2 quarts (2 L) warm water

3 bay leaves

2 tablespoons red wine vinegar

To serve

Crusty bread

A simple lentil soup is a classic in most cuisines, but this Balkan soup is actually one of the most well-known and popular winter dishes among the Greeks. It is a rich, hearty, and satisfying soup made with brown or green lentils, which are very common in Greece, cooked with a drizzle of red wine vinegar to enhance the flavor. Some cook the lentils separately until they are soft and only then add them to the soup, but I think it's best to cook them with all the other ingredients to give the soup a deeper flavor. And of course, it also means one less pot to clean. Do not leave out the dried oregano, which adds a wonderful aroma and flavor.

Rinse the lentils in a fine-mesh sieve under cold water until the water runs clear, and drain.

In a large nonstick pot, heat the olive oil over medium heat. Add the onion, carrots, and celery, and cook for 6 to 8 minutes, stirring occasionally, until the vegetables are soft and fragrant.

Add the tomato paste, oregano, chili flakes (if using), salt, and pepper, and sauté for 1 minute.

Add the lentils and cook, stirring constantly, for 1 minute, until the lentils are coated in the oil and tomato paste, shiny and warm.

Add the water and bay leaves and stir. Bring to a boil over high heat, reduce the heat to low, cover the pot, and cook for 40 to 45 minutes, until the lentils are tender. Use a slotted spoon to skim off the foam throughout the cooking.

Add the vinegar and stir. If the soup is too thick, add boiling water until it reaches your desired consistency. Taste and adjust the seasoning, if needed.

Remove and discard the bay leaves. Ladle the soup into individual bowls and serve immediately with crusty bread.

Leftover fakes soupa can be stored in an airtight container in the refrigerator for up to 4 days.

Bean Soup

FASOLADA

Serves 6 to 8

2 cups (340 g) dried white beans, preferably cannellini or navy beans, soaked overnight

⅓ cup (80 ml) extra-virgin olive oil

1 large onion, finely chopped

2 medium carrots, cut into ¼-inch (6 mm) cubes

2 celery stalks, cut into ¼-inch (6 mm) cubes

6 garlic cloves, finely chopped

2 quarts (2 L) warm water

One 14-ounce (400 g) can crushed tomatoes

3 bay leaves

1 heaping teaspoon dried oregano

½ to 1 teaspoon dried chili flakes (optional)

Kosher salt and freshly ground black pepper to taste

3 tablespoons lemon juice

¼ cup (6 g) finely chopped fresh flat-leaf parsley

To serve

Crusty bread

Fasolada, sometimes called the national food of the Greeks, is a hearty dish, enjoyed during the colder months of the year. Greeks often credit this soup with helping people survive during difficult periods in history. Today, in monasteries open to the public, visitors may be treated to a bowl of fasolada, often served with a slice of bread and wine made by the monks or nuns.

In traditional recipes, the beans are cooked in water and then the rest of the ingredients are added. Instead, this recipe uses the Italian technique for sofrito: sautéing all the vegetables in olive oil before adding the rest of the ingredients. This way, the soup is richer and more concentrated. It's best served warm with cold feta crumbled on top and good bread on the side. The beans must soak in water overnight or for at least 8 hours, so be sure to plan ahead.

Rinse the beans in a fine-mesh sieve under cold water until the water runs clear, and drain.

In a large nonstick pot, heat the olive oil over medium heat. Add the onion, carrots, celery, and garlic, and cook for 6 to 8 minutes, stirring occasionally, until the vegetables are soft and fragrant.

Add the beans, water, crushed tomatoes, bay leaves, oregano, chili flakes (if using), salt, and pepper, and stir. Bring to a boil over high heat, reduce the heat to low, cover the pot, and cook for 60 to 80 minutes, until the beans are tender. Use a slotted spoon to skim off the foam throughout the cooking.

Add the lemon juice and parsley and stir. If the soup is too thick, add boiling water until it reaches your desired consistency. Taste and adjust the seasoning, if needed.

Remove and discard the bay leaves. Ladle the soup into individual bowls and serve immediately with crusty bread alongside.

Leftover fasolada can be stored in an airtight container in the refrigerator for up to 4 days.

Tomato and Orzo Soup

MANESTRA

Serves 4 to 6

¼ cup (60 ml) extra-virgin olive oil

1 large onion, finely chopped

3 or 4 garlic cloves, finely chopped

2 tablespoons tomato paste

1 teaspoon dried oregano

½ to 1 teaspoon dried chili flakes (optional)

Kosher salt and freshly ground black pepper to taste

6 ripe medium tomatoes, cut into ¼-inch (6 mm) cubes

6 cups (1.4 L) warm water

1 teaspoon sugar

1 cup (180 g) uncooked orzo

To serve

3 ounces (85 g) feta, coarsely crumbled

Orzo is a pasta shaped like a grain of rice; it's made from durum wheat flour. The Greek name for orzo is kritharaki, which means "little barley." The Greeks cook orzo in sauces or soups like this tomato-based recipe. In the past, this simple and satisfying delicacy was a good breakfast to sustain workers during the long hours on the land. Today manestra is appreciated as a healthy, nutritious, and cost-effective soup that is just as popular with children as with adults.

In a medium nonstick pot, heat the olive oil over medium heat. Add the onion and garlic and cook for 5 to 6 minutes, stirring occasionally, until the onion and garlic are soft and fragrant.

Add the tomato paste, oregano, chili flakes (if using), salt, and pepper, and sauté for 1 minute.

Add the tomatoes with their juices, water, and sugar, and stir. Bring to a boil over high heat, reduce the heat to low, cover the pot, and cook for 15 to 20 minutes, until the tomatoes are soft.

Add the orzo. Bring to a boil again and cook uncovered for 8 to 10 minutes, until the orzo is soft.

If the soup is too thick, add boiling water until it reaches your desired consistency. Taste and adjust the seasoning, if needed.

Ladle the soup into individual bowls, sprinkle with the feta, and serve immediately.

Leftover manestra can be stored in an airtight container in the refrigerator for up to 4 days.

Lemon Chicken Soup

KOTOSOUPA AVGOLEMONO

Serves 4 to 6

½ cup (90 g) uncooked short-grain rice, preferably arborio or carnaroli

¼ cup (60 ml) extra-virgin olive oil

1 medium onion, finely chopped

1 large carrot, cut into ¼-inch (6 mm) cubes

1 celery stalk, cut into ¼-inch (6 mm) cubes

2 or 3 garlic cloves, finely chopped

6 cups (1.4 L) warm chicken stock

1 boneless, skinless chicken breast (1 pound/450 g), cut in half

2 or 3 bay leaves

2 or 3 thyme sprigs

Kosher salt and freshly ground black pepper to taste

2 large eggs

1 tablespoon cornstarch

1 tablespoon lemon zest

⅓ cup (80 ml) lemon juice

To serve

2 tablespoons chopped fresh dill

The Greeks believe this soup can cure everything from the common cold to heartache. It differs in composition and texture from other chicken soups thanks to the addition of rice or orzo and an egg mixture called avgolemono. This sauce-like addition of eggs whisked with lemon lends the soup a velvety rich texture. Don't skip the step of tempering the egg mixture before adding it to the soup, or else you'll end up with scrambled egg bits in the soup.

Rinse the rice in a fine-mesh sieve under cold water until the water runs clear, and drain.

In a large nonstick pot, heat the olive oil over medium heat. Add the onion, carrot, celery, and garlic, and cook for 6 to 8 minutes, stirring occasionally, until the vegetables are soft and fragrant.

Add the stock, chicken, bay leaves, thyme, salt, and pepper, and stir. Bring to a boil over high heat, reduce the heat to low, cover the pot, and cook for 7 to 8 minutes, until the chicken is cooked through.

Use tongs to transfer the chicken pieces to a bowl and set aside until they are cool enough to handle.

Meanwhile, add the rice to the pot and cook for 10 minutes.

Once the chicken has cooled, use your hands or two forks to shred the meat and set aside.

Turn off the heat. Remove and discard the bay leaves and thyme sprigs. Remove ¾ cup (180 ml) of the cooking liquid from the pot and place it in a small bowl. Set aside.

Whisk the eggs with the cornstarch in a clean medium bowl. Add the lemon zest and lemon juice and whisk well to combine. To temper the eggs, add the reserved ¾ cup (180 ml) of the hot cooking liquid to the egg mixture and whisk quickly so the eggs don't cook.

Pour the egg sauce into the pot and stir. Add the shredded chicken and stir again. Bring to a gentle boil over medium heat to let the

flavors combine and to cook the eggs through, and immediately turn off the heat. Taste and adjust the seasoning, if needed.

Ladle the soup into individual bowls, sprinkle with the dill, and serve immediately.

Leftover kotosoupa avgolemono can be stored in an airtight container in the refrigerator for up to 3 days.

Meatball Soup

YOUVARLAKIA AVGOLEMONO

Serves 4 to 6

7 cups (1.7 L) chicken or beef stock

2 or 3 bay leaves

2 or 3 thyme sprigs

Kosher salt and freshly ground black pepper to taste

½ cup (90 g) uncooked short-grain rice, preferably arborio or carnaroli

1 pound (450 g) ground chuck

1 small onion, finely chopped

3 or 4 garlic cloves, finely chopped

1 large egg

½ cup (12 g) finely chopped fresh flat-leaf parsley

1 tablespoon extra-virgin olive oil

3 egg yolks

1 tablespoon cornstarch

1 tablespoon lemon zest

⅓ cup (80 ml) lemon juice

To serve

2 tablespoons chopped fresh dill

Soft, juicy meatballs made with ground beef, rice, onion, and lots of herbs are cooked in chicken broth. The avgolemono—a lemon and egg sauce that is added when the meatballs are ready— upgrades and enriches the soup.

In a medium nonstick pot, bring the stock, bay leaves, and thyme sprigs to a boil over medium-high heat. Taste and adjust the seasoning, if needed. Turn off the heat and set aside.

Rinse the rice in a fine-mesh sieve under cold water until the water runs clear, and drain.

Transfer the rice to a large bowl, add the ground beef, onion, garlic, egg, parsley, olive oil, salt, and pepper, and mix with your hands.

Do a taste test. Return the stock to a boil and cook a tiny portion of the meat mixture in it for 2 minutes. Taste and adjust the seasoning, if needed. Turn off the heat.

Moisten your hands with water to keep the mixture from sticking to them. Use your hands to scoop out about a flat tablespoon of the meat mixture and shape it into a 1½-inch (4 cm) ball. Place the meatball on a plate or a tray. Repeat until you have used up all the meat mixture; you should have about 24 meatballs.

Return the stock to medium heat and carefully add the meatballs one by one to the stock. Once again, bring to a boil, reduce the heat to low, cover the pot, and cook for 30 minutes, until the meatballs are cooked through.

Turn off the heat. Remove and discard the bay leaves and thyme sprigs. Remove ¾ cup (180 ml) of the hot cooking liquid from the pot and place it in a small bowl. Set aside.

Whisk the egg yolks with the cornstarch in a clean medium bowl. Add the lemon zest and lemon juice and whisk well to combine. To temper the eggs, add the reserved ¾ cup (180 ml) of the hot cooking liquid to the egg yolk mixture and whisk quickly so the egg yolks don't cook.

(recipe continues)

Pour the egg yolk mixture into the pot and stir. Bring to a gentle boil over medium heat to let the flavors combine and to cook the egg yolks through, and immediately turn off the heat. Taste and adjust the seasoning, if needed.

Ladle the soup into individual bowls, sprinkle with the dill, and serve immediately.

Leftover youvarlakia avgolemono can be stored in an airtight container in the refrigerator for up to 3 days.

Spinach Rice

SPANAKORIZO

Serves 4 to 6

1 cup (180 g) uncooked short-grain rice, preferably arborio or carnaroli

⅓ cup (80 ml) extra-virgin olive oil

1 medium onion, finely chopped

2 scallions (white and light green parts only), thinly sliced

½ cup coarsely chopped fresh dill

1 teaspoon kosher salt

½ teaspoon freshly ground black pepper

2½ cups (600 ml) warm water

½ pound (225 g) fresh spinach, well rinsed and coarsely chopped

To serve

¼ cup (60 ml) lemon juice

3 tablespoons extra-virgin olive oil

The texture of spanakorizo is reminiscent of Italian risotto, although the preparation is much simpler and doesn't require standing next to the pot and constantly stirring. Spanakorizo is tied to one of the most famous traditions in Greece, the ancient carnival in Tyrnavos, a town in the Peloponnese region. Each year on the first Monday of Lent, the people of Tyrnavos participate in a parade in honor of Dionysus, the god of wine and festivities. The carnival attracts thousands of visitors and includes elaborate costumes, masks, and music. During the celebrations, the local version of spanakorizo, called burani, is made.

Rinse the rice in a fine-mesh sieve under cold water until the water runs clear, and drain. Set aside.

In a medium nonstick pot, heat the ⅓ cup (80 ml) olive oil over medium heat. Add the onion, scallions, and dill, and cook for 6 to 8 minutes, stirring occasionally, until the vegetables are soft and fragrant.

Add the rice, salt, and pepper and cook, stirring constantly, for 1 minute, until the rice is coated in the oil, shiny and warm.

Add the water and stir. Bring to a boil over high heat, reduce the heat to low, cover the pot, and simmer for 12 minutes, until most of the water is absorbed. The rice should be slightly undercooked.

Place the spinach on top of the rice (don't stir it in) and cover the pot. Cook for 5 minutes, until the spinach starts to wilt.

Stir the spinach into the rice, re-cover the pot, and cook for another 3 to 4 minutes, until the rice is tender and the spinach is wilted and loses its volume.

Turn off the heat and let rest covered for 10 minutes before serving.

Drizzle with the lemon juice and the 3 tablespoons olive oil and serve immediately.

The rice is best if served shortly after cooking, but leftover spanakorizo can be stored in an airtight container in the refrigerator for up to 4 days and reheated in the microwave.

Rice with Vegetables

PILAFI ME LAHANIKA

Serves 8 to 10

2 cups (320 g) uncooked basmati rice

6 tablespoons (90 g) extra-virgin olive oil

½ cup (65 g) pine nuts

1 large onion, finely chopped

2 medium carrots, coarsely grated

2 teaspoons kosher salt

1 heaping teaspoon freshly ground black pepper

1 teaspoon ground cinnamon

½ cup (65 g) small black raisins (also called Zante currants)

3½ cups (840 ml) warm water

Every Greek household has its own version of pilaf made with rice or bulgur. This is the recipe I make for every holiday or festive meal as a wonderful side for meat, chicken, or fish. It is enriched with vegetables, pine nuts, and raisins, and seasoned with lots of black pepper and ground cinnamon.

Rinse the rice in a fine-mesh sieve under cold water until the water runs clear, and drain. Set aside.

In a medium nonstick pot, heat 3 tablespoons of the olive oil over medium heat. Add the pine nuts and toast, stirring occasionally, for 2 to 3 minutes, until golden. Transfer the pine nuts to a bowl. Set aside.

In the same pot, heat the remaining 3 tablespoons olive oil. Add the onion and carrots and cook for 6 to 8 minutes, stirring occasionally, until the vegetables are soft and fragrant.

Add the rice, salt, pepper, and cinnamon, and cook, stirring constantly, for 1 minute, until the rice is coated in the oil, shiny and warm.

Add the toasted pine nuts, raisins, and water, and stir. Bring to a boil, reduce the heat to low, and cook covered for 18 minutes, until the rice is tender. Do not stir or open the pot during cooking.

Turn off the heat and let rest covered for 10 minutes before serving.

Fluff the rice with a fork, transfer to a serving bowl, and serve immediately.

The rice is best if served shortly after cooking, but leftover pilafi can be stored in an airtight container in the refrigerator for up to 4 days and reheated in the microwave.

Variations

- Instead of pine nuts, use blanched sliced almonds.

- Instead of 2 carrots, use 1 small sweet potato.

- Instead of black raisins, use halved dried cranberries.

Okra in Tomato Sauce

BAMIES LATHERES ME DOMATES

Serves 4 to 6

1 pound (450 g) fresh okra

1 cup (240 ml) vinegar

2 cups (480 ml) cold water

6 tablespoons extra-virgin olive oil

1 medium onion, finely chopped

3 or 4 garlic cloves, finely chopped

2 tablespoons tomato paste

4 ripe medium tomatoes, cut into ¼-inch (6 mm) cubes

2 cups (480 ml) warm water

1 teaspoon sugar

Kosher salt and freshly ground black pepper to taste

To serve

Crusty bread

Okra tends to elicit love or hate, but rarely indifference. The Greeks are completely in favor of okra, and in order to counter the vegetable's sometimes slimy texture, they soak it in vinegar and then dry it in the sun. Trays of okra sunbathing for hours on the terraces and roofs of homes are a common sight in Greece on Wednesdays and Fridays, when the Greek Orthodox don't eat meat and enjoy more vegetables than usual. In this recipe, the okra is soaked in vinegar for a few minutes, dried, then lightly fried in olive oil. It gives almost the same result as sun-drying the okra, but in much less time. This okra dish is a terrific vegan side, but one that could stand on its own as a main.

Using a paring knife, carefully cut off the okra stems. Be careful not to cut into the okra itself; otherwise it will become slimy.

Transfer the trimmed okra to a large bowl. Add the vinegar and cold water, mix, and let rest for 15 minutes.

Rinse the okra under cold water and drain. Dry with a paper towel.

In a medium nonstick pot, heat 3 tablespoons of the olive oil over medium-high heat. Add the okra and fry for 3 to 4 minutes, until the okra starts to turn golden. Use a slotted spoon to transfer the okra to a medium bowl and set aside.

In the same pot, heat the remaining 3 tablespoons olive oil over medium heat. Add the onion and garlic and cook for 5 to 6 minutes, stirring occasionally, until the onion and garlic are soft and fragrant.

Add the tomato paste and sauté for 1 minute.

Add the fried okra, the tomatoes with their juices, the water, sugar, salt, and pepper, and stir. Bring to a boil, reduce the heat to low, cover the pot, and simmer for 30 to 40 minutes, until the okra is tender but not mushy. Taste and adjust the seasoning, if needed.

Serve the braised okra hot or at room temperature with crusty bread.

Leftover bamies can be stored in an airtight container in the refrigerator for up to 4 days.

Roasted Vegetables

BRIAM

Serves 6 to 8

¼ cup (60 ml) plus 3 tablespoons extra-virgin olive oil

1 medium onion, finely chopped

One 14-ounce (400 g) can crushed tomatoes

1½ teaspoons dried oregano

Kosher salt and freshly ground black pepper to taste

1 long and narrow globe eggplant, cut into ¼-inch (6 mm) rounds

4 or 5 Roma tomatoes, cut into ¼-inch (6 mm) rounds

1 large zucchini, cut into ¼-inch (6 mm) rounds

4 medium Yukon Gold or russet potatoes, peeled and cut into ¼-inch (6 mm) rounds

Briam is a colorful vegan Greek casserole of summer vegetables roasted in olive oil. This dish is similar to the French ratatouille, except that here the vegetables are usually cut larger rather than diced, and they keep their shape at the end of cooking. You can cook briam on the stove or in the oven, and it can include almost any vegetables you wish: tomatoes, zucchini, potatoes, eggplant, okra, carrots, sweet potatoes, bell peppers, and more. Another name for this dish in Greece is tourlou, which means "everything mixed together," indicating the ease and flexibility of this dish. And because of its simplicity, briam is one of the first foods that Greeks learn to cook. It evokes family life in the villages and is very popular among urbanites and Greeks living abroad who crave a taste of home.

Preheat the oven to 350°F (175°C).

In a medium nonstick pan, heat 3 tablespoons of the olive oil over medium heat. Add the onion and cook, stirring occasionally, for 5 to 6 minutes, until the onion is soft and fragrant.

Add the crushed tomatoes, 1 teaspoon of the oregano, salt, and pepper, and stir. Bring to a boil and turn off the heat. Taste and adjust the seasoning, if needed.

Pour the tomato sauce into a 12-inch (30 cm) round glass or metal baking dish and spread evenly.

Arrange the vegetables on top of the sauce, overlapping them and alternating slices of eggplant, tomato, potato, and zucchini, working from the outside of the pan to the center.

Drizzle the remaining ¼ cup (60 ml) olive oil on top and sprinkle with the remaining ½ teaspoon oregano, salt, and pepper.

Bake uncovered for 35 to 45 minutes, until the briam is golden brown and the vegetables are cooked through. Serve immediately.

Leftover briam can be stored in an airtight container in the refrigerator for up to 4 days. To reheat, warm in the oven at 325°F (160°C) for 10 minutes.

Boiled Wild Leafy Greens

HORTA

Serves 2 to 4

1 heaping tablespoon kosher salt, plus more to taste

1⅓ pounds (600 g) chard or kale

3 tablespoons extra-virgin olive oil

3 tablespoons lemon juice

Throughout winter and into spring, Greece is abundant with wild greens, called horta, that grow on the hillsides and in the mountains. During this period, you can see people gathering greens to make this dish. Hundreds of different edible greens grow wild in Greece, and to someone who is not a local, they are likely to look like weeds. Horta is therefore known as a hidden or secret treasure, and there is a common belief that the best wild horta grows in places far from human habitation. Most of the greens Greeks use for horta are not available outside the country, but don't despair—you can make this dish with chard, kale, beet greens, spinach, chicory, or other leafy greens. It is served warm or at room temperature as a kind of salad or side for a main dish.

Fill a large pot with water and season with the 1 heaping tablespoon salt. Bring to a boil.

Use a sharp knife to remove the chard leaves from the thick ribs (you can leave thin ribs). Discard the ribs and roughly chop the leaves. Add the chard leaves to the boiling water and cook for 5 to 15 minutes, until the leaves are tender but not mushy. Drain well.

Place the leaves on a serving plate. Drizzle with the olive oil and lemon juice and season with salt. Serve warm or at room temperature.

Leftover horta can be stored in an airtight container in the refrigerator for up to 5 days.

TRADITIONAL FOODS AND GREEK CEREMONIES

Many customs and religious ceremonies in Greece involve symbolic culinary products and foods, from olive oil and honey to roasted lamb and salt cod. Greeks use specific dishes to mark life's milestones, such as baptisms, weddings, or funerals. The recipes for such traditional foods are often passed down from generation to generation and reflect the diverse culinary traditions of the country.

Baptisms are major social events, a cause for celebration and a time of sweetness for adults and kids alike. In Soufli, a town in the region of Thrace in northern Greece, the birth of a child is announced to relatives and godparents with gifts of custard pie, wine, and sweet bread. During the baptismal ceremony, the godparents cover the baby's body with olive oil, which is meant to protect the child from temptation and sin, a custom that evolved from a practice of ancient Grecian wrestlers, who lathered themselves with olive oil to slip from the grasp of their opponents. Throughout the country, christenings are marked by festivities in which Greeks enjoy sweets like sugared fruits, baklava, fried honeyed dough, syrup-covered pastries, macaroons sprinkled with powdered sugar, semolina halva, and pies. Guests at a christening are given small decorated boxes or pouches containing almonds coated with hardened sugar, known as dragées. These dragées are always packed in even numbers, symbolizing the desire for this happy event to be repeated in the future through the birth of another child.

Dragées are given as gifts in wedding ceremonies as well. These sugar-coated Jordan almonds are ripe with symbolism. Their egg shape represents fertility and their white color stands for purity. Their sweetness symbolizes the joys of marriage, and their hardness stands for the difficulties of life. In contrast to the practice in christenings, the number of dragées handed out at weddings is always an odd number, symbolizing indivisibility. In many places, upon entering

FIVE

MAINS

Traditionally, Greeks eat their largest meal late in the evening, around eight or nine. Dinner usually consists of a main dish—grilled fish, meats, or poultry—and vegetable side dishes. Some Greeks, however, prefer to make their midday meal their largest, preparing some of these main dishes for a plentiful lunch.

The sea surrounds Greece for thousands of kilometers, and its bounty feeds the people of Greece, who embrace the abundance it has to offer. At sunrise, fishermen return to the beach to sell their catch from the night to restaurants and fish markets or shops.

Those living close to the coast often directly employ a fisherman to catch fresh fish for the evening meal.

Unlike the French, who like to serve their fish with rich, heavy sauces, the Greeks keep it simple. They let the natural flavors of the fish shine through, and most of the time they are satisfied with a drizzle of lemon juice and olive oil, as with their classic fried fish (page 182). For a light main dish that can also be served as a complete meal, fish is baked in a bed of tomato and vegetable sauce (page 185), and for special occasions, whole fish are baked in coarse salt (page 189).

Meat and poultry dishes are considered symbols of the good life in Greek culture. However, the consumption of animal protein was not as widespread in the past as it is today. Until the end of the 1950s, meat was expensive and reserved for holiday meals and Sundays; it was never served more than twice a week. Just as vegetables are enjoyed seasonally in Greek cuisine, so are specific meats. For example, pork is consumed mostly in winter. Partridges and hare were once eaten in Greece, usually during the winter months, when other meats were scarce. However, game meats are not so common today. Stifado, a well-known and comforting winter stew that originally featured wild rabbit, is made today mainly from beef (page 205).

Since meat was expensive, Greeks found ways to expand their main dishes by adding vegetables, pastas, and grains. Some examples of this include Moussaka (page 211) and Pastitsio (page 214). Both dishes are often served at special occasions, but they are revered as classic comforts of homecoming as well.

Greeks don't like to waste food, so animals have long been consumed from nose to tail (even before the term was known), as in the recipe for Greek Roasted Chicken over Lemon Potatoes (page 191).

Fried Fish

PSARI TIGANITO

Serves 4 to 6

1⅔ pounds (750 g) whitefish fillet, such as cod, sea bass, or sea bream

Kosher salt and freshly ground black pepper to taste

2 large eggs

¾ cup (95 g) all-purpose flour

¾ cup (180 ml) extra-virgin olive oil

To serve

1 lemon, cut into wedges

Tzatziki (page 25)

Simple and delicious fried fish is popular throughout Greece. The fish is typically a whitefish, such as cod, sea bass, or sea bream, that is filleted and then coated, fried in olive oil, and served with lemon wedges. The most common method is to coat the fish in flour, egg, and bread crumbs, but there are many other variations. Some people soak the fish in milk before frying it to soften the flavor, while others prefer to coat the fish in batter or a mixture of flour and bread crumbs. I prefer an egg-and-flour coating, without bread crumbs, which creates a crispy crust without overwhelming the delicate flavor of the fish.

Ask the fishmonger to fillet the fish for you. At home, cut the fillets to your desired size.

Remove the fish from the refrigerator about 20 minutes before frying to bring it close to room temperature.

Rinse the fish in a colander and pat dry with a paper towel.

Cut the fish into 2-inch (5 cm) pieces. Season the fish pieces with salt and pepper.

Whisk the eggs in a shallow medium bowl. Place the flour in another shallow bowl.

Working with one piece at a time, dip the fish pieces in the egg, lift them out, let them drip for a second, and then dredge them in the flour, coating them well, and shake off any excess flour. Set aside on a clean plate.

Cover the bottom of a medium nonstick pan with olive oil about ½ inch (12 mm) deep, and bring to a frying temperature over medium heat. You can check the temperature of the oil by dipping the handle of a wooden spoon in it. When the oil is ready, it will gently sizzle and bubble up around the handle.

Line a plate with a paper towel.

Working in batches, fry 5 or 6 fish pieces at a time for 2 to 3 minutes on each side, until the fish is golden all over, using tongs to turn the fish.

Transfer the fried fish to the paper towel–lined plate. Repeat with the rest of the fish pieces.

Serve immediately with lemon wedges and tzatziki.

Leftover fried fish can be stored in an airtight container in the refrigerator for up to 3 days. To reheat, warm in the oven at 325°F (160°C) for 6 to 8 minutes.

Fish in Tomato Sauce

PSARI PLAKI

Serves 2 to 4

2 medium whole whitefish (about 1½ pounds/700 g each), such as sea bass, snapper, or branzino, gutted, cleaned, and scaled

¼ cup (60 ml) plus 3 tablespoons extra-virgin olive oil

1 medium onion, finely chopped

3 medium Yukon Gold or russet potatoes, cut into ½-inch (12 mm) cubes

2 medium fennel bulbs, cut into ½-inch (12 mm) cubes

5 ripe medium tomatoes, cut into ½-inch (12 mm) cubes

½ cup (80 g) pitted Kalamata olives

⅓ cup (80 ml) ouzo or dry white wine

⅓ cup (80 ml) warm water

1 heaping tablespoon tomato paste

1 teaspoon dried oregano

Kosher salt and freshly ground black pepper to taste

To serve

2 tablespoons coarsely chopped fresh flat-leaf parsley

1 lemon, cut into wedges

The name psari plaki translates literally to "fish plate," *plaki* referencing the shallow dish traditionally used to bake this fish in a simple tomato sauce. I like to add ouzo to give it a taste of anise, and potatoes and fennel to make it an even more substantial and satisfying main course. The result is an excellent combination of crispy fish and soft and juicy vegetables. Psari plaki is typically made on Palm Sunday and on March 25, Greece's National Day of Independence, which is why Greeks affectionately call it their "national fish dish."

Remove the fish from the refrigerator about 30 minutes before baking to bring it close to room temperature. Rinse the fish in a colander and pat dry with a paper towel.

In a large nonstick skillet, heat 3 tablespoons of the olive oil over medium heat. Add the onion and cook for 5 to 6 minutes, stirring occasionally, until the onion is soft and fragrant. Transfer the cooked onion to a small bowl.

Preheat the oven to 400°F (200°C).

Add the remaining ¼ cup (60 ml) olive oil, the potatoes, and the fennel to the same skillet, and sauté for 6 to 8 minutes over medium-high heat, until the potatoes and fennel are golden. Add the cooked onion, tomatoes, olives, ouzo, water, tomato paste, oregano, salt, and pepper, and mix.

Bring to a boil, reduce the heat to low, and simmer uncovered for 8 to 10 minutes, until the vegetables are tender but not mushy.

Taste and adjust the seasoning, if needed.

Transfer the cooked vegetables to a 9-by-13-inch (23 by 33 cm) glass or metal baking dish or a 13-inch (33 cm) round baking dish.

Cut 6 to 8 slits ¼ inch (6 mm) deep in the exposed side of each fish. Place the fish on top of the vegetables slitted-side up, and season the fish with salt and pepper.

(recipe continues)

Bake uncovered for 20 to 25 minutes, until the fish are golden and the skin separates easily from the flesh. At the end of baking, you can set the oven to broil and brown the fish on top.

Sprinkle the chopped parsley on top and serve immediately with lemon wedges.

TOMATOES

Tomatoes are stars in Greek cuisine. They have been cultivated in Greece since the sixteenth century, but because they were considered poisonous at that time, they were mostly grown as ornamental plants and used to decorate gardens and homes. At the beginning of the nineteenth century, Franciscan monks planted tomato seeds in the garden of a monastery in Athens, and from that point on, they became staples in the Greek menu.

The Greek government has a program to promote the growing of tomatoes in Greece by providing farmers with financial assistance and technical support. The island of Santorini is known for its excellent tomatoes, which are small, thick-skinned, and intensely flavored. This is due to the island's sandy and dry volcanic soil.

Here are some tips for choosing tomatoes:

- Look for tomatoes that are whole and firm, without bruises or blemishes. The skin should be smooth and shiny.

- Avoid tomatoes that are soft or have wrinkled skin, which indicates they are overripe.

- Smell the tomato. A ripe tomato will have a sweet and fruity smell.

Salt-Baked Whole Fish

OLOKLIRO PSARI ME ALATI

Serves 2 to 4

2 whole whitefish
(about 1⅔ pounds/750 kg each),
such as sea bass, snapper, or
branzino, gutted and cleaned,
scales intact

1 medium lemon, cut into ¼-inch
(6 mm) rounds

¾ cup (20 g) thyme leaves
(from about 20 sprigs), plus
4 whole sprigs

9 pounds (4 kg) coarse salt

2 cups (480 ml) water

To flambé

½ cup (120 ml) ouzo

To serve

¼ cup (60 ml) lemon juice

¼ cup (60 ml) extra-virgin
olive oil

Kosher salt and freshly ground
black pepper to taste

Gorgeous salt-baked fish can be found in all the seaside restaurants of Greece. It's a dramatic moment when the waiter flames the fish with ouzo in front of the diners, then cracks the salt crust to present the juicy fillets. At home, this dish is surprisingly easy to make, if somewhat messy. And though it's a fun and impressive technique, you can skip the flambé if it's too much for you.

Use a firm-fleshed whitefish, such as sea bass. The salt crust helps keep the fish moist and flavorful. Ask the fishmonger to clean and gut the fish but not to remove the scales. This way the salt will not penetrate the fish but instead enclose it like a casing. To make this recipe, you will need a large quantity of coarse salt: For every 1⅔ pounds (750 g) of fish, you will need 4½ pounds (2 kg) of coarse salt. If you want to bake more fish, scale up the amount of salt according to the number of fish.

Remove the fish from the refrigerator about 30 minutes before baking to bring it close to room temperature.

Rinse the fish in a colander and pat dry with a paper towel.

Preheat the oven to 350°F (175°C). Line a sheet pan with parchment paper.

Fill the cavity of each fish with a few lemon slices and 2 thyme sprigs.

In a large bowl, mix the coarse salt, water, and thyme leaves until the salt feels like wet sand.

For each fish, place about one-sixth of the salt mixture on the prepared sheet pan, in an oblong shape resembling the silhouette of the fish, large enough to hold the fish. Arrange a fish on top of each base, and cover with the rest of the salt mixture. Using your hands, pack the salt mixture onto the fish by pushing and squeezing the salt into the fish, so that the whole fish is well covered.

Bake for 35 minutes (after about 20 minutes, the salt will have hardened, but continue baking so that the fish can cook through). If you're using smaller or larger fish, you'll need to adjust the cooking time: For 1½-pound (680 g) fish, bake for 30 minutes; for 2-pound (900 g) fish, bake for 40 minutes.

(recipe continues)

Remove the fish from the oven and immediately pour the ouzo over the fish and light with a long match or kitchen torch. Let it flambé until the flames subside.

Using a knife, cut through the salt crust and gently remove it. Discard the salt. Extract the fish from the salt, remove the skin, take out the flesh, and transfer to a plate.

Drizzle the fish with the lemon juice and olive oil, season with salt and pepper, and serve immediately.

Greek Roasted Chicken over Lemon Potatoes

OLOKLIRI KOTA STI SKARA

Serves 4 to 6

1 medium whole
(3½ to 4 pounds/1.6 kg)
roasting chicken

1 tablespoon lemon zest

⅓ cup (80 ml) lemon juice,
from at least 1 lemon cut in half
(reserve the squeezed lemon
halves)

⅓ cup (80 ml) extra-virgin
olive oil

1 tablespoon dried oregano

Kosher salt and freshly ground
black pepper to taste

6 to 8 medium waxy potatoes,
scrubbed and cut into 6 wedges

If you are looking for a chicken dish that will be a hit with the family, this is it. Before Jamie Oliver brought lemon chicken to the world, the Greeks had been preparing it for centuries. Olokliri kota sti skara is mentioned in Greek literature as early as the sixteenth century, and it has probably been cooked in Greece for even longer.

This dish most likely originated in the Peloponnese region, where there is a long tradition of grilling meat and vegetables. It is typically made with a fire-roasted whole chicken covered in a mixture of olive oil, lemon juice, and dried oregano and roasted over an open flame or in the oven (for home cooking) until golden brown on the outside and juicy on the inside. The crispy potatoes absorb all the wonderful juices of the chicken.

To roast the chicken, start with the breast up. Halfway through the roasting time, turn the chicken breast-down. This will help keep the breast juicy and prevent it from drying out. You can use the leftover chicken to make sandwiches the next day.

Remove the chicken from the refrigerator about 45 minutes before roasting to bring it close to room temperature. This will ensure that the chicken cooks evenly. Pat the chicken dry with a paper towel.

Preheat the oven to 350°F (175°C).

Place the chicken in a 9-by-13-inch (23 by 33 cm) roasting pan.

In a small bowl, whisk together the lemon zest, lemon juice, olive oil, and oregano.

Stuff the 2 squeezed lemon halves inside the chicken's cavity. Tie the legs together with kitchen twine to help the chicken hold its shape. Pour two-thirds of the lemon mixture over the chicken (reserve one-third of it for the potatoes). Season with salt and pepper and use your hands to massage the juices into the chicken so that the whole chicken is covered with the lemon mixture. Place the chicken breast-side up. Roast uncovered for 35 minutes, until the chicken is golden on top.

(recipe continues)

Meanwhile, in a large bowl, mix the potatoes and the rest of the lemon mixture. Season with salt and pepper and toss to coat the potatoes in the juices.

Remove the pan from the oven. Arrange the potatoes around the chicken. Using large tongs, turn the chicken breast-side down, and roast uncovered for another 45 minutes, until the potatoes and chicken are golden brown all over and the chicken is cooked through inside; an instant-read thermometer inserted in the thickest part of the thigh should read 165°F (74°C).

Let the chicken rest for 10 minutes before carving and serving with the potatoes on the side.

Leftover chicken and potatoes can be stored in an airtight container in the refrigerator for up to 3 days. To reheat, warm in the oven at 325°F (160°C) for 10 to 15 minutes.

Chicken Stew over Pasta

PASTITSADA

Serves 4 to 6

4 bone-in, skin-on chicken thighs

Kosher salt and freshly ground black pepper to taste

⅓ cup (80 ml) plus 2 tablespoons extra-virgin olive oil

1 medium onion, finely chopped

1½ cups (360 ml) warm water

One 14-ounce (400 g) can crushed tomatoes

2 cinnamon sticks

2 bay leaves

1 heaping teaspoon sugar

1 heaping teaspoon sweet or hot paprika

1 teaspoon ground cumin

½ teaspoon freshly ground nutmeg

½ teaspoon ground cloves

1 pound (450 g) bucatini

To serve

3 tablespoons coarsely chopped fresh flat-leaf parsley

Grated Parmesan

Pastitsada is a hearty and delicious chicken and pasta dish from the island of Corfu, made with pieces of chicken cooked in a rich tomato sauce flavored with cinnamon, cumin, nutmeg, paprika, and cloves. The bucatini is cooked separately, so it doesn't overcook, and then served with the chicken stew and grated Parmesan.

Remove the chicken thighs from the refrigerator about 30 minutes before roasting to bring them close to room temperature.

Pat the chicken dry with a paper towel. Season with salt and pepper.

In a wide nonstick pot, heat ⅓ cup (80 ml) of the olive oil over high heat. Add the chicken thighs and sear for 4 to 5 minutes on each side, until they are golden brown. Transfer the chicken to a large bowl.

Reduce the heat to low, add the onion, and cook for 4 to 5 minutes, stirring occasionally, until the onion is soft and fragrant.

Add the water, crushed tomatoes, cinnamon sticks, bay leaves, sugar, paprika, cumin, nutmeg, cloves, salt, and pepper to the pot, mix, and bring to a boil over high heat. Taste and adjust the seasoning, if needed.

Return the seared chicken to the pot and gently shake the pot so that most of the chicken is covered by the sauce. Once again, bring to a boil, then reduce the heat to low, cover the pot, and simmer for 60 minutes, using tongs to turn the chicken over in the sauce about every 20 minutes. Remove the lid and cook for another 10 to 15 minutes, until the chicken is tender and cooked through and the sauce is thick. Taste and adjust the seasoning, if needed. Remove and discard the cinnamon sticks and bay leaves.

Fill a separate large pot with water and season with 2 tablespoons salt. Bring to a boil.

Add the pasta to the boiling water and cook according to the package instructions until the pasta is al dente.

Drain the pasta and transfer to a large serving bowl. Add the remaining 2 tablespoons olive oil and stir.

Remove the chicken pieces from the tomato sauce, then add the tomato sauce to the pasta and toss to combine. Place the chicken on top, sprinkle with the parsley and Parmesan, and serve immediately.

The pasta is best if served shortly after cooking, but leftover pastitsada can be stored in an airtight container in the refrigerator for up to 3 days and reheated in the microwave.

Chicken Souvlaki

SOUVLAKI KOTOPOULO

Serves 4 to 6

⅓ cup (80 ml) plus 2 tablespoons extra-virgin olive oil

1 teaspoon lemon zest

¼ cup (60 ml) lemon juice

1 heaping teaspoon dried oregano

1 heaping teaspoon kosher salt

½ teaspoon freshly ground black pepper

2 pounds (900 g) boneless, skinless chicken thighs, cut into 1½-inch (4 cm) pieces

To serve

Pita

4 or 6 whole leaves of lettuce such as iceberg or butter lettuce

2 ripe medium tomatoes, cut into ½-inch (12 mm) cubes

1 small red onion, halved and thinly sliced

3 tablespoons coarsely chopped fresh flat-leaf parsley

Full-fat Greek yogurt or Tzatziki (page 25)

Anyone who visits Greece, even for a short weekend, has eaten these skewered boneless chicken morsels sold at every street food stall and restaurant. Chicken thighs are cut into cubes and soaked in a marinade of olive oil, lemon juice, and dried oregano, which softens the meat and enhances its flavor. Souvlaki is typically grilled over an open flame, but it can also be cooked in a pan on the stovetop. It is usually served with pita, tomatoes, onions, and tzatziki.

If you are using wood skewers and a grill, soak the skewers in water for 30 minutes so they don't burn while grilling. Grilling on a griddle pan doesn't require soaking the skewers.

In a large bowl, whisk together ⅓ cup (80 ml) of the olive oil, the lemon zest, lemon juice, oregano, salt, and pepper. Add the chicken pieces and toss to coat all the chicken in the marinade. Let sit for at least 20 minutes. If you marinate it longer, cover the bowl with plastic wrap and place it in the refrigerator. Remove from the refrigerator about 30 minutes before grilling to bring it close to room temperature.

Thread 5 or 6 chicken pieces on each skewer.

Heat a charcoal or gas grill or a griddle pan over high heat. Brush the grill or the pan with the remaining 2 tablespoons olive oil to prevent the chicken from sticking.

Place the chicken skewers on the grill or the pan and cook for 3 to 4 minutes on each side, until the chicken is golden brown all over and cooked through.

Serve the skewers immediately with the pita, lettuce, tomatoes, red onion, parsley, and yogurt.

Lamb Souvlaki

SOUVLAKI ARNI

Serves 4 to 6

⅓ cup (80 ml) plus 2 tablespoons extra-virgin olive oil

¼ cup (60 ml) orange juice

¼ cup (60 ml) ouzo

1 heaping teaspoon dried oregano

1 heaping teaspoon kosher salt

½ teaspoon freshly ground black pepper

2 medium red onions, cut into quarters

2 medium red bell peppers, halved, cored, seeded, and cut into 1⅓-inch (3.5 cm) chunks

1⅔ pounds (750 g) lamb shoulder, cut into 1⅓-inch (3.5 cm) pieces

To serve

Pita (optional)

Full-fat Greek yogurt or Tzatziki (page 25; optional)

Lamb souvlaki—skewered meat—is one of the most popular street foods in Greece. In fact, there are many eating establishments called souvlatzidika that specialize in serving different kinds of souvlakis. My version of lamb souvlaki is prepared in a wonderful marinade of olive oil, orange juice, ouzo, and dried oregano. It softens the meat and gives it a flattering sweetness when grilled with chunks of red onion and bell peppers.

If you are using wood skewers and a grill, soak the skewers in water for 30 minutes so they don't burn while grilling. Grilling on a griddle pan doesn't require soaking the skewers.

In a large bowl, whisk together ⅓ cup (80 ml) of the olive oil, the orange juice, ouzo, oregano, salt, and black pepper.

Separate the onion quarters into pieces of 2 layers. Add the onion pieces and the bell peppers to the bowl with the marinade. Add the lamb pieces and toss to coat all the lamb and vegetables in the marinade. Let sit for at least 20 minutes. If you marinate it longer, cover the bowl with plastic wrap and place it in the refrigerator. Remove from the refrigerator about 30 minutes before grilling to bring it close to room temperature.

Thread 4 lamb pieces on each skewer, alternating chunks of red onion and bell pepper between the meat.

Heat a charcoal or gas grill or a griddle pan over high heat. Brush the grill or the pan with the remaining 2 tablespoons olive oil to prevent the lamb from sticking.

Place the lamb skewers on the grill or the pan and cook for 3 to 5 minutes on each side, until the lamb is golden brown and cooked according to your preference.

Serve the skewers immediately with pita and yogurt, if using.

Meatballs in Tomato Sauce with Olives

SOUTZOUKAKIA ME ELIES

Serves 6 to 8

1⅓ pounds (600 g) ground beef

½ cup (50 g) bread crumbs

1 large egg

1 medium onion, finely chopped

½ cup (12 g) finely chopped fresh flat-leaf parsley

1 teaspoon dried oregano

1 teaspoon dried mint

Kosher salt and freshly ground black pepper to taste

½ cup (120 ml) extra-virgin olive oil

2⅓ cups (560 ml) water

One 28-ounce (800 g) can crushed tomatoes

1⅓ cups (200 g) green olives

2 tablespoons tomato paste

1 teaspoon sugar

½ to 1 teaspoon dried chili flakes (optional)

To serve
Cooked rice, pasta, or potatoes

The name soutzoukakia comes from the Greek word *soutsouki*, which means "sausage." However, the meatballs in this dish are made with ground beef or lamb and cooked in a tomato sauce.

In a large bowl, use your hands to mix the ground beef, bread crumbs, egg, onion, parsley, oregano, mint, salt, and pepper.

Do a taste test. In a large nonstick pan with a little oil, fry a tiny portion of the meat mixture. Taste and adjust the seasoning, if needed. Don't wash the pan; you'll use it to fry all the meatballs.

Moisten your hands with a little water and scoop out about a flat tablespoon of the meat mixture and shape it into a 1½-inch (4 cm) ball. Place the meatball on a clean plate or a tray. Repeat until you have used up all the meat mixture; you should have about 30 meatballs.

Line a plate with a paper towel. Heat the olive oil in the same large nonstick pan over medium-high heat. Add the meatballs and sear for 2 to 3 minutes on each side, until golden brown all over, using tongs to turn them. Remove the seared meatballs from the pan and let them drain on the paper towel–lined plate.

In a medium pot, mix the water, crushed tomatoes, olives, tomato paste, sugar, chili flakes (if using), salt, and pepper, and bring to a boil over high heat. Taste and adjust the seasoning, if needed.

Add the seared meatballs to the pot and gently shake the pot so that all the meatballs are covered in sauce. Once again, bring to a boil, reduce the heat to low, cover the pot, and simmer for 30 minutes, until the meatballs are tender and cooked through. Taste and adjust the seasoning, if needed.

Serve warm with rice.

Leftover meatballs and sauce can be stored in an airtight container in the refrigerator for up to 3 days. To reheat, cook on the stovetop over medium heat for 10 to 15 minutes.

Beef Stew with Shallots

STIFADO

Serves 4 to 6

3 pounds (1.4 kg) beef shoulder, cut into 2-inch (5 cm) chunks

½ cup (120 ml) extra-virgin olive oil

16 whole shallots, peeled

Kosher salt and freshly ground black pepper to taste

2 cups (480 ml) dry red wine

3 cups (720 ml) warm water

7 or 8 garlic cloves, sliced ⅛ inch (3 mm) thick

3 tablespoons tomato paste

3 or 4 bay leaves

1 heaping teaspoon sugar

1 heaping teaspoon ground cinnamon

The French have beef bourguignon and the Greeks have stifado—a rich stew with tender chunks of beef, red wine, and shallots. It is best to make the dish a day before and let it rest overnight.

Remove the beef from the refrigerator about 1 hour before cooking to bring it close to room temperature.

In a wide nonstick pot, heat ¼ cup (60 ml) of the olive oil over medium-high heat. Add the shallots and sauté for 4 to 5 minutes, until the shallots are golden. Transfer the sautéed shallots to a medium bowl.

Season the beef chunks with salt and pepper.

Add the remaining ¼ cup (60 ml) olive oil to the pot. Working in batches, add half of the beef chunks and sear for 3 to 4 minutes on each side, until the beef is brown all over. Transfer the seared meat to a large bowl. Repeat with the rest of the beef.

Add the wine to the pot and bring to a boil over high heat. Reduce the heat to medium and simmer uncovered for 10 minutes, until the wine has reduced by half, to about 1 cup.

Add the water, garlic, tomato paste, bay leaves, sugar, cinnamon, salt, and pepper. Stir and bring to a boil over high heat. Taste and adjust the seasoning, if needed.

Return the seared meat to the pot and gently shake the pot so that all the meat is covered in sauce. Once again, bring to a boil, reduce the heat to low, cover the pot, and simmer for 90 minutes.

Add the sautéed shallots to the pot and mix. Once again, bring to a boil over high heat, reduce the heat to low, cover the pot, and simmer for another 90 minutes, until the meat is very tender and cooked through. Remove and discard the bay leaves. Taste and adjust the seasoning, if needed.

Serve warm.

Leftover stifado can be stored in an airtight container in the refrigerator for up to 3 days.

Veal Stew

SOFRITO

Serves 4 to 6

2 pounds (900 g) boneless veal knuckle (round roast)

Kosher salt and freshly ground black pepper to taste

⅓ cup (40 g) all-purpose flour

½ cup (120 ml) plus 3 tablespoons extra-virgin olive oil

7 or 8 garlic cloves, sliced ⅛ inch (3 mm) thick

2 cups (480 ml) chicken or beef stock

⅓ cup (80 ml) dry white wine

¼ cup (60 ml) white wine vinegar

To serve

2 tablespoons coarsely chopped fresh flat-leaf parsley

Roasted potatoes or cooked rice

The name sofrito comes from the Italian word *soffritto*, which means "lightly fried" or "slightly sautéed." The usage of the word in Greece likely dates to the fifteenth century, when the island of Corfu was under Venetian rule. The Venetians brought their cooking techniques to the island, one of which was to coat meat with flour and fry it before cooking in sauce. As with this stew, frying the meat provides a crispy coating and also enriches and thickens the sauce. Sofrito is typically served with potatoes or rice, but it can also be served with pasta or bread.

Remove the veal from the refrigerator about 1 hour before cooking to bring it close to room temperature.

Cut the veal into ½-inch (12 mm) slices. Season the veal slices with salt and pepper.

Place the flour in a wide shallow bowl. Working with one slice at a time, dredge the veal slices in the flour, coating them well, and shake off any excess flour. Set aside on a clean plate.

Cover the bottom of a large nonstick pan with ½ cup (120 ml) of the olive oil so that it's about ¼ inch (6 mm) deep, and bring to a frying temperature over medium-high heat. You can check the temperature of the oil by dipping the handle of a wooden spoon in it. When the oil is ready, it will gently sizzle and bubble up around the handle.

Add half of the veal slices and sear for 2 to 3 minutes on each side, until the veal is golden brown all over, using tongs to turn it. Transfer the seared veal to a large bowl and repeat with the rest of the veal.

In a medium nonstick pot, heat the remaining 3 tablespoons olive oil over low heat. Add the garlic and fry for 10 to 20 seconds, stirring constantly, until the garlic starts to turn golden. Be careful not to brown the garlic.

Add the stock, wine, vinegar, salt, and pepper, mix, and bring to a boil over high heat.

Add the seared veal to the pot and gently shake the pot so that all the veal is covered in sauce. Once again, bring to a boil, reduce the

heat to low, cover the pot, and simmer for 90 minutes, until the veal is tender and cooked through. Taste and adjust the seasoning, if needed.

Sprinkle the parsley on top and serve immediately with roasted potatoes.

Leftover sofrito can be stored in an airtight container in the refrigerator for up to 3 days. To reheat, cook on the stovetop over medium heat for 10 to 15 minutes.

Roast Lamb Shoulder

KLEFTIKO

Serves 4 to 6

1 medium (about 6½ pounds/
3 kg) lamb shoulder, bone in

1 tablespoon lemon zest

⅓ cup (80 ml) lemon juice

⅓ cup (80 ml) extra-virgin
olive oil

3 or 4 bay leaves

1 heaping tablespoon dried
oregano

Kosher salt and freshly ground
black pepper to taste

6 to 8 medium waxy potatoes,
scrubbed and cut into 6 wedges

Kleftiko is the crown jewel of Greek meat dishes, suitable to serve on holidays and special occasions. This one derives its name from *klephtes*, meaning "thieves and rebels," who during the Ottoman occupation would steal sheep or goats and cook the meat in sealed clay pots buried in underground pits so as to keep the smoke of an open fire from betraying their locations. The secret to a tender, juicy lamb kleftiko is a long, slow roasting of the lamb in its own juices and with olive oil and lemon juice. You start with a high oven heat for 30 minutes and then reduce the heat, cooking it for a few hours, until the meat is very tender and falls off its bone. Since the potatoes are done faster than the lamb, they are added to the oven during the second half of the roasting.

Remove the lamb from the refrigerator about 2 hours before roasting to bring it close to room temperature. Place the lamb in a roasting pan large enough to easily accommodate it.

Preheat the oven to 400°F (200°C).

In a small bowl, mix the lemon zest, lemon juice, olive oil, bay leaves, and oregano.

Pour two-thirds of the lemon mixture over the lamb (reserve one-third of it to be used later for the potatoes). Season with salt and pepper and use your hands to massage the juices into the lamb so that the whole lamb is covered with the lemon mixture.

Roast the lamb uncovered for 25 to 30 minutes, until it starts to turn golden brown.

Remove the pan from the oven and cover the pan with aluminum foil. Reduce the oven heat to 350°F (175°C), and return the covered pan to the oven. Bake for another 90 minutes.

Meanwhile, in a large bowl, mix the potatoes and the rest of the lemon mixture. Season with salt and pepper and toss to coat the potatoes in the juices.

(recipe continues)

Remove the pan from the oven and take off the foil. Arrange the potatoes around the lamb, cover with the foil, and return the covered pan to the oven.

Bake for another 90 to 120 minutes, until the lamb is tender and falling off the bone and the potatoes are tender. You can remove the aluminum foil for the last 20 minutes of roasting to brown the lamb and potatoes, if you'd like. Remove and discard the bay leaves and let the lamb rest for 10 minutes before carving and serving.

Leftover kleftiko can be stored in an airtight container in the refrigerator for up to 3 days. To reheat, warm in the oven at 325°F (160°C) for 15 to 20 minutes.

Eggplant and Potato Casserole

MOUSSAKA

Serves 12 to 16

For the vegetables

3 medium eggplants, peeled vertically with zebra-like stripes, and sliced into ½-inch (12 mm) rounds

6 to 8 tablespoons (90 to 120 ml) extra-virgin olive oil

Kosher salt and freshly ground black pepper to taste

5 medium potatoes, sliced into ¼-inch (6 mm) rounds

For the meat sauce

3 tablespoons extra-virgin olive oil

1 medium onion, finely chopped

3 or 4 garlic cloves, finely chopped

1½ pounds (700 g) ground chuck or lamb (or half and half)

¾ cup (180 ml) dry red wine

3 tablespoons tomato paste

One 14-ounce (400 g) can crushed tomatoes

1 cup (240 ml) warm water

3 bay leaves

1 heaping teaspoon dried oregano

1 heaping teaspoon ground cinnamon

Kosher salt and freshly ground black pepper to taste

For the béchamel and assembly

⅓ cup (75 g) butter, cut into cubes

½ cup (65 g) all-purpose flour

Moussaka is a baked dish of fried potatoes and eggplant, and sometimes zucchini, layered with a spiced lamb sauce and creamy béchamel sauce. Its preparation is a small labor of love, so moussaka is mostly served on special occasions such as celebrations or welcoming friends and loved ones. But this deliciously rich homemade version is far more satisfying than the flavorless attempts found at touristy restaurants. To lighten the dish, I don't fry the potatoes and eggplant but instead bake them in the oven before layering them with the sauces. It's easier, less messy, and healthier, too. Moussaka can be made a day in advance and is even better the next day, after the flavors have melded in the fridge.

Prepare the vegetables: Preheat the oven to 350°F (175°C). Line four sheet pans with parchment paper, or you can use two pans twice.

Arrange the eggplant rounds on two prepared sheet pans, drizzle with 4 to 5 tablespoons olive oil, and sprinkle with salt and pepper. Roast the eggplant in the oven for 35 to 40 minutes, until tender and golden but not mushy.

On the other two sheet pans, or on the same two lined with new sheets of parchment, arrange the potato rounds, drizzle with 2 to 3 tablespoons olive oil, and sprinkle with salt and pepper. Roast the potatoes for 30 to 35 minutes, until tender and golden but not mushy.

Prepare the meat sauce: While the vegetables are roasting, heat the 3 tablespoons olive oil in a large nonstick pan over medium heat. Add the onion and garlic and cook for 5 to 6 minutes, stirring occasionally, until the onion and garlic are soft and fragrant.

Add the ground meat and cook, stirring and breaking up the meat, for 4 to 6 minutes, until it loses its pink color.

Add the wine to the pan, bring to a boil over medium-high heat, and cook for 4 to 6 minutes, until the wine has evaporated.

(ingredients continue)

(recipe continues)

4 cups (960 ml) whole milk

¼ teaspoon freshly ground nutmeg

¼ teaspoon kosher salt, plus more to taste

2 large eggs

1 cup (100 g) finely grated Parmesan

Add the tomato paste, crushed tomatoes, water, bay leaves, oregano, cinnamon, salt, and pepper, and mix. Bring to a boil over high heat, reduce the heat to low, and cook uncovered for 30 to 35 minutes, until most of the liquid has evaporated, leaving a thick sauce. Taste and adjust the seasoning, if needed.

Turn off the heat and set aside. Remove and discard the bay leaves.

Prepare the béchamel: In a medium pot over low to medium-low heat, melt the butter. Add the flour and cook for 10 to 20 seconds, stirring constantly with a wooden spoon to create a roux.

Gradually pour the milk into the pot while whisking constantly. Add the nutmeg and the ¼ teaspoon salt and cook over medium-high heat for another 2 to 4 minutes, still whisking, until the sauce thickens. Turn off the heat.

Whisk the eggs in a medium bowl. To temper the eggs, add about ¾ cup (180 ml) of the hot béchamel sauce to the eggs and stir immediately. Pour the warm egg mixture back into the pot with the béchamel and stir. Add ½ cup (50 g) of the Parmesan and stir until the sauce is smooth and thick. Taste and adjust the seasoning, if needed.

Assemble and bake the moussaka: In a 9-by-13-inch (23 by 33 cm) glass or ceramic baking dish, arrange the baked potato rounds evenly in a single layer. Sprinkle ¼ cup (25 g) of the Parmesan evenly over the potatoes. Next, add a single layer of the baked eggplant rounds, and pour the meat sauce evenly over the eggplant. Place another layer of eggplant slices and sprinkle the remaining ¼ cup (25 g) Parmesan on top. Pour the béchamel sauce evenly over the top.

Bake uncovered for 30 to 40 minutes, until the moussaka is golden brown and bubbling. Let rest for 15 minutes before cutting and serving.

Leftover moussaka can be stored in an airtight container in the refrigerator for up to 3 days. To reheat, warm in the oven at 325°F (160°C) for 10 to 15 minutes.

Baked Pasta with Meat and Béchamel Sauce

PASTITSIO

Serves 12 to 16

For the meat sauce

¼ cup (60 ml) extra-virgin olive oil

1 medium onion, finely chopped

1 medium carrot, cut into ¼-inch (6 mm) cubes

1 celery stalk, cut into ¼-inch (6 mm) cubes

3 to 4 garlic cloves, finely chopped

1½ pounds (700 g) ground beef or lamb (or half and half)

1 cup (240 ml) dry red wine

2 tablespoons tomato paste

One 28-ounce (800 g) can crushed tomatoes

1 cup (240 ml) water

3 bay leaves

3 cinnamon sticks

Kosher salt and freshly ground black pepper to taste

For the pasta

2 tablespoons plus ½ teaspoon kosher salt

1 pound (450 g) bucatini, penne, or ziti

2 tablespoons extra-virgin olive oil

8 ounces (225 g) feta, coarsely crumbled

½ teaspoon freshly ground black pepper

When the Venetians conquered the Ionian islands between the fourteenth and eighteenth centuries, many local dishes in the area were influenced by Italian cuisine. In the sixteenth century, Venetian pastitsio was a tall and luxurious pastry made of sweet dough that enveloped pasta and meat. It was a true spectacle to impress guests. Almost four centuries later, perhaps inspired by that version of the dish, chef Nikolaos Tselementes ditched the pastry format and created the modern pastitsio. The recipe appeared in Tselementes's cookbook *Greek Cookery* (published in 1950), which introduced elements of French cuisine, such as the use of butter and cream, that were not part of Greek cuisine before. Without Tselementes, dishes like this one and Moussaka (page 211) would not include the wonders of béchamel sauce. Today pastitsio is a popular dish in Greece and is often served as a main course or party dish.

Prepare the meat sauce: In a large nonstick pan, heat the ¼ cup (60 ml) olive oil over medium heat. Add the onion, carrot, celery, and garlic, and cook for 8 to 10 minutes, stirring occasionally, until the vegetables are soft and fragrant.

Add the ground meat and cook by stirring and breaking up the meat for 4 to 6 minutes, until the meat loses its pink color.

Add the wine to the pan, bring to a boil over medium-high heat, and cook for 4 to 6 minutes, until the wine has evaporated.

Add the tomato paste, crushed tomatoes, water, bay leaves, cinnamon sticks, salt, and pepper, and mix. Bring the mixture to a boil over high heat, reduce the heat to low, and cook uncovered for 30 to 40 minutes, until most of the liquid has evaporated, leaving a thick sauce. Taste and adjust the seasoning, if needed.

Remove the pan from heat. Remove and discard the bay leaves and cinnamon sticks.

For the béchamel

⅓ cup (75 g) butter,
cut into cubes

½ cup (65 g) all-purpose flour

4 cups (960 ml) whole milk

¼ teaspoon freshly ground
nutmeg

¼ teaspoon kosher salt

2 large eggs

½ cup (50 g) finely grated
Parmesan

Prepare the pasta: Fill a large pot with water and season with 2 tablespoons salt. Bring to a boil.

Add the pasta and cook for 2 minutes less than the package instructions call for. The pasta should be slightly undercooked.

Drain the pasta and transfer to a large bowl. Add 2 tablespoons olive oil and mix.

Add the feta, 1 cup of the meat sauce, ½ teaspoon salt, and the pepper to flavor the pasta, and mix. Layer the pasta mixture evenly into a 9-by-13-inch (23 by 33 cm) glass or ceramic baking dish, and pour the rest of the meat sauce evenly over the pasta.

Preheat the oven to 350°F (175°C).

Prepare the béchamel: In a medium pot over low to medium-low heat, melt the butter. Add the flour and cook for 10 to 20 seconds, stirring constantly with a wooden spoon to create a roux.

Gradually pour the milk into the pot while whisking constantly. Add the nutmeg and the ¼ teaspoon salt and cook over medium-high heat for another 2 to 4 minutes, still whisking, until the sauce thickens. Turn off the heat.

Whisk the eggs in a medium bowl. To temper the eggs, add about ¾ cup (180 ml) of the hot béchamel sauce to the eggs and stir immediately. Pour the warm egg mixture back into the pot with the béchamel and stir. Add the Parmesan and stir until the sauce is smooth and thick. Taste and adjust the seasoning, if needed.

Pour the béchamel sauce evenly over the pasta.

Bake uncovered for 30 to 40 minutes, until the pastitsio is golden brown and bubbling. Let rest for 15 minutes before cutting and serving.

Leftover pastitsio can be stored covered in the refrigerator for up to 3 days. To reheat, warm in the oven at 325°F (160°C) for 10 to 15 minutes.

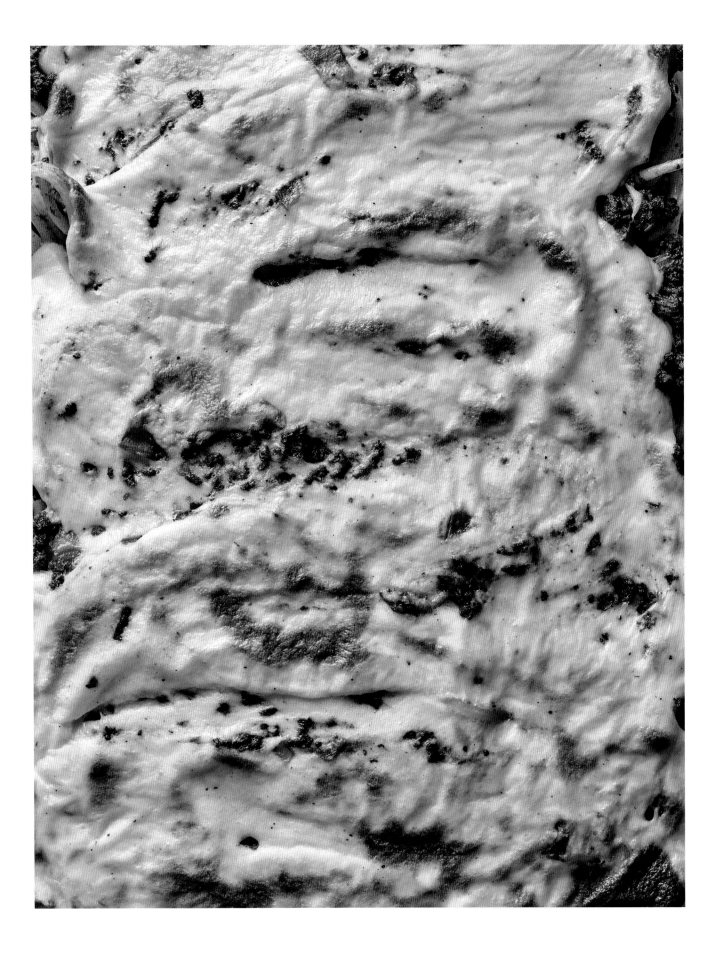

THE LAND OF GOATS AND SHEEP

There are as many goats as people in Greece, and half as many sheep. On the island of Samothrace, there are forty-five goats for every person. Sheep and goats are used to produce cheese, meat, milk, and wool. A fourth of the milk produced in the country comes from goats, and almost half of all meat production comes from goats and sheep.

The earliest evidence for pastoral activities in Greece comes from the island of Crete around 8,500 years ago. Shortly afterward, the Greek mainland saw the emergence of nomadic pastoralism, in which the entire community travels with their flocks from winter to summer pastures and vice versa. Some pastoral communities in the Epirus area of western Greece still follow this way of life today. People began to breed sheep for their wool around 7,000 years ago, and by the Bronze Age, wool and linen, along with leather, became the main clothing materials in the Greek world.

While wool, cheese, and milk from goats and sheep were common in ancient Greece, the meat of these animals was considered a delicacy, prepared for special events, religious ceremonies, and festivals. The ancient Greeks celebrated their dead by roasting goats and lambs over hearths, drinking wine, and dancing in the belief that their departed loved ones were there to share in their joy.

In Greece, a single goat horn, known as the Horn of Amalthea, is a symbol of abundance. According to mythology, baby Zeus, king of the gods, was nursed and protected by a nymph named Amalthea, who took the form of a goat. One day, as Zeus was playing, he accidentally broke one of Amalthea's horns. To make up for this mishap, the child god blessed the broken horn so it would always be filled with whatever its owner desired.

In the Greek Orthodox religion, the Easter lamb symbolizes Christ and his message of resurrection. Although the practice dates to pre-Christian times, nothing says Greek Easter like the custom of spit-roasting a goat on Easter Sunday, a technique that Greeks call souvla. The gyro, a sandwich made by wrapping pita around roasted meats, usually lamb or a combination of lamb and other meats, is the most popular street food in Greece today. It's also one of the best-known ambassadors of Greek cuisine, popular all over the world.

Today rural Greece is filled with grazing goats and flocks of sheep, led by the herders through the rolling meadows and mountains. One might even see boats in the Aegean Sea filled with sheep and goats traveling with their shepherds to small, uninhabited islets, which provide new pastures for grazing. Sightings of these roaming herds are often accompanied by a distant ringing sound, the jingling of the metal bells attached to the animals. Since ancient times, shepherds have used the sound of these bells to track their sheep and goats. Today, for many Greeks, this jingling conjures up memories of the beautiful countryside.

SIX

SWEETS

While there are many well-known Greek pastries and sweets, Greeks do not recognize the concept of dessert. A typical Greek meal will usually end with a plate of fresh seasonal fruit. Instead, sweet treats are served in the afternoon alongside a strong coffee and a glass of cold water. The country is full of sweet pastry shops called zaharoplastia, which means "confectionery." And for celebrations or special occasions, it is customary to bring a box of treats from the local zaharoplastia as a gift to friends and family.

Greeks enjoy a myriad of sweets, from bite-size confectionery like Marzipan (page 224) to custards such as Rice Pudding (page 247) and cookies like Kourabiedes (page 227), the famous almond butter cookies. Cakes and pastries are usually in the style of siropiasta, which is a term used to describe pastries soaked in honey or sugar syrup to moisten the crumb. Perhaps the most famous siropiasta, of course, is Baklava (page 239), which is widely popular among the Greeks but actually originated in modern-day Turkey. Like many treats enjoyed in Greece, including Loukoumades (page 244)—fried doughnuts—baklava was brought to the country during the long Ottoman rule.

To enjoy a range of fruits and vegetables throughout the year, Greeks preserve seasonal produce at their peak. Recipes like Sweet Orange Peel Preserve (page 250) or Cherry Spoon Preserve (page 253) would most traditionally be served in a spoon for a simple sweet bite—hence the name spoon sweets. They are a custom of Greek hospitality, presented to guests on a silver tray to welcome them into one's home. However, my own favorite way to enjoy these preserves is spooned over thick Greek yogurt.

Many Greek pastries are sweetened with honey and flavored with nuts and spices. Honey is a treasured ingredient, deeply tied to Greek mythology and history (see page 261). It was used in Greece long before the arrival of sugar and is the star ingredient in treats like Pasteli (page 249), a very simple honey and sesame bar. Walnuts, almonds, pistachios, and sesame seeds add texture to cakes and cookies, while common spices like cinnamon, clove, nutmeg, and cardamom bring a warm and inviting flavor to Karidopita (page 236), a spiced walnut cake. Quinces Baked in Red Wine (page 256) are an example of how Greek confections are often a beautiful balance of sweet, nutty, and warm flavors.

Marzipan (Almond Paste)

AMIGDALOPASTA

Makes about 60 pieces

2 cups (280 g) whole raw almonds

1¼ cups (150 g) powdered sugar

3 to 4 tablespoons water

2 teaspoons rosewater

Everyone makes their homemade marzipan a little differently: soaking the almonds or not, mixing ground almonds with simple syrup instead of sugar, adding egg whites or just water. I prefer to make marzipan the easy way, just as my Greek grandmother taught me. I use whole almonds that are already peeled, and I grind them in a food processor. Don't use pre-ground almonds. Crushing the almonds releases the fresh oil, which glues everything together and also creates a fresher and tastier marzipan, so there's no need to add almond extract. As a plus, this version just so happens to be vegan, too.

Place the almonds in the bowl of a food processor and grind for about 1 minute, until the almonds turn into a fine powder, similar to almond flour. Turn off the food processor.

Add the powdered sugar and process for 10 seconds, just until the almond powder and powdered sugar mix together. Add 3 tablespoons of the water and the rosewater and process for about 1 minute, until the mixture forms into a paste similar to the texture of Play-Doh. If the mixture is too dry and doesn't hold together, add another tablespoon of water and process for 10 to 20 seconds. Be careful not to add too much water; otherwise the mixture will turn into an almond spread. If it is too runny, add a tablespoon or two of almond flour.

Remove the blade from the food processor and use your hands to carefully scoop out the almond paste and shape it into a ball.

On a clean work surface, cut the almond paste into 4 even pieces. Roll one piece into a rope about 1¼ inches (3 cm) in diameter. Using a sharp knife, cut the rope diagonally into diamond-shaped pieces ¾ inch (2 cm) thick. Repeat with the rest of the almond paste.

Marzipan can be stored in an airtight container in the refrigerator for up to 7 days or in the freezer for up to a month.

Almond Butter Cookies

KOURABIEDES

Makes about 45 cookies

⅔ cup (150 g) butter, at room temperature

2 cups (250 g) all-purpose flour

1 cup (115 g) almond flour

1¼ cups (150 g) powdered sugar, plus ½ cup (65 g) for coating

1 heaping teaspoon baking powder

1 large egg

2 tablespoons ouzo or another favorite liqueur

The word *koura* is Arabic and means both "ball" and "almond." These almond ball cookies arrived in Greece from the Middle East during the Ottoman period and became the traditional dessert for Christmas and the New Year's celebrations, but today they are served all year round. My grandmother used to store her version in a large tin box and hide it in strange places, but we would always find the stash and quickly devour the buttery cookies. The telltale indication was our clothes ended up all powdered in white. I've upgraded Grandma's dough with a shot of ouzo, which gives the cookies a delicate and lovely aniseed flavor. If you don't like ouzo, you can replace it with any other liqueur.

Preheat the oven to 350°F (175°C). Line two baking sheets with parchment paper.

In a stand mixer fitted with the paddle attachment, combine the butter, all-purpose flour, almond flour, 1¼ cups (150 g) of the powdered sugar, the baking powder, egg, and ouzo on medium-low speed for 2 to 3 minutes, just until the dough is uniform, smooth, and slightly sticky. Don't overknead the dough or the cookies will be tough after baking.

Use your hands to scoop out about half a tablespoon of the cookie mixture and shape it into a 1¼-inch (3 cm) ball, weighing ½ ounce (15 g). Then flatten the dough ball slightly and set it on one of the prepared baking sheets. Repeat until you have used up all the cookie dough, spacing the cookies at least 1 inch (2.5 cm) apart.

Bake one pan at a time for 8 to 12 minutes, just until the cookies are light golden. Let cool to room temperature on the pan.

Use a sifter to dust the cooled cookies with the remaining ½ cup (65 g) powdered sugar.

Kourabiedes can be stored in an airtight container at room temperature for up to 2 weeks.

Gluten-Free Almond Cookies

AMIGDALOTA

Makes about 24 cookies

1 egg white from a large egg

1¾ cups (200 g) almond flour

¾ cup (95 g) powdered sugar, plus ⅓ cup (40 g) for dusting

1 teaspoon baking powder

1 tablespoon rosewater

24 whole cloves

These easy-to-make almond cookies contain only six ingredients and are gluten-free. In Greece, they are often served or gifted for engagements, weddings, baptisms, and birthday celebrations, as they symbolize happy news, family joy, and good luck. Since they are flourless, Greek Jews make them for Passover, too. Be careful not to overbake the cookies so that their insides remain soft and chewy.

Preheat the oven to 350°F (175°C). Line a baking sheet with parchment paper.

In a large bowl, whisk the egg white for 1 minute, until foam starts to form.

Add the almond flour, ¾ cup (95 g) of the powdered sugar, the baking powder, and the rosewater, and stir with a spoon. When the dough becomes difficult to stir, knead with your hands until the mixture forms into a paste similar to the texture of Play-Doh.

Use your hands to scoop out about half a tablespoon of the cookie mixture and shape it into a 1¼-inch (3 cm) ball. Then mold the dough ball into the form of a small pear. Repeat until you have used up all the cookie dough.

Place the remaining ⅓ cup (40 g) powdered sugar in a shallow bowl. Roll the pear-shaped cookies in the powdered sugar, coating them well. Stick a whole clove on top of each cookie, to resemble a pear stem.

Arrange the cookies on the prepared baking sheet, spacing them at least ¾ inch (2 cm) apart.

Bake for 8 to 12 minutes, just until the cookies are light golden. Let cool to room temperature on the pan.

Amigdalota can be stored in an airtight container at room temperature for up to 2 weeks.

Semolina No-Bake Cake

HALVAS SIMIGDALENIOS

Makes one 8-inch (20 cm) bundt pan

For the syrup

4 cups (960 ml) water

3 cups (600 g) sugar

3 tablespoons lemon juice

6 whole cloves

2 cinnamon sticks

For the cake

¾ cup (75 g) blanched sliced almonds

1 cup (240 ml) light olive oil or vegetable oil

2 cups (340 g) semolina flour

1 tablespoon orange zest

1 teaspoon ground cinnamon

In the United States, halva typically refers to a fudge-like sesame confection. But the word *halva* is actually a general term for sweets in Turkish, so you can find all kinds of confections that go by this name in Balkan kitchens. This is a vegan no-bake treat made of semolina flour, olive oil, and a sugar syrup, scented with cinnamon and cloves and enriched with almonds.

Prepare the syrup: In a medium saucepan, mix together the water, sugar, lemon juice, cloves, and cinnamon sticks. Bring to a boil over medium heat, reduce the heat to low, and simmer uncovered for about 5 minutes, until the sugar dissolves completely and the syrup is clear. Let cool to room temperature. Remove and discard the cloves and cinnamon sticks. Set aside.

Prepare the cake: Heat a large nonstick pot over medium heat. Put the almonds in the pot and toast, stirring constantly with a wooden spoon, for 2 to 3 minutes, until the almonds are lightly golden. Transfer the toasted almonds to a bowl. Set aside.

To the same pot, add the oil and semolina flour and cook over medium heat, stirring occasionally with a wooden spoon, for 10 to 12 minutes, until the semolina flour has turned golden. Remove the pot from the heat. Add the orange zest and ground cinnamon and mix well. Pour the reserved syrup into the semolina mixture, add the toasted almonds, and stir to combine. Return the pot to the stove and bring to a boil over medium-high heat. Reduce the heat to medium-low and cook, stirring constantly with a wooden spoon, for 10 to 12 minutes, until the mixture is very thick and pulls away from the sides of the pot.

Pour the mixture into a nonstick 8-inch (20 cm) bundt pan and use a spoon to spread it evenly throughout the pan. Tap the pan on the work surface to knock any air bubbles out of the mixture. Smooth the surface with the back of a spoon. Let cool to room temperature.

Invert the dessert onto a serving plate or cake stand. Serve at room temperature.

Halvas simigdalenios can be stored covered at room temperature for up to 3 days.

Semolina Cake with Orange Syrup

REVANI

Makes one 8-by-12-inch (20 by 30 cm) cake

For the syrup

1½ cups (300 g) sugar

1 cup (240 ml) water

1 tablespoon orange zest

½ cup (120 ml) orange juice

2 cinnamon sticks

For the cake

½ cup (120 ml) plus 1 tablespoon vegetable oil

5 large eggs

1 teaspoon vanilla extract

¼ teaspoon salt

1 cup (200 g) sugar

1 cup (170 g) semolina flour

1 cup (125 g) all-purpose flour

1 heaping teaspoon baking powder

1 heaping teaspoon baking soda

Revani is a wonderful example of a siropiasta, a category of syrup-soaked cakes and pastries. Here the sugar syrup is enriched with orange zest and juice to give the cake a bright citrus flavor, and the cake has a lovely grainy texture thanks to the semolina flour.

Prepare the syrup: In a medium saucepan, mix together the sugar, water, orange zest, orange juice, and cinnamon sticks. Bring to a boil over medium heat, reduce the heat to low, and simmer uncovered for about 5 minutes, until the sugar dissolves completely and the syrup is clear. Turn off the heat and let cool to room temperature. Remove and discard the cinnamon sticks.

Prepare the cake: Preheat the oven to 350°F (175°C). Grease an 8-by-12-inch (20 by 30 cm) glass or ceramic baking dish with 1 tablespoon of the oil.

In a large bowl, whisk the eggs. Add the remaining ½ cup (120 ml) oil, the vanilla, and the salt, and whisk to combine.

In a medium bowl, mix together the sugar, semolina flour, all-purpose flour, baking powder, and baking soda. Add the flour mixture to the egg mixture and mix with a wooden spoon until the batter is smooth and uniform. Pour the batter into the prepared baking dish and smooth the surface.

Bake for 25 to 30 minutes, until the cake is golden and a toothpick inserted in the center comes out clean but slightly damp.

Remove the cake from the oven and immediately poke the top of the cake 12 to 16 times with a toothpick or a wooden skewer. Pour the reserved syrup evenly over the top of the cake. Let cool to room temperature in the pan while the cake absorbs the syrup. Serve in the pan or slice into individual pieces.

Revani can be stored covered at room temperature for up to 3 days.

Walnut Cake

KARIDOPITA

Makes one 9-inch (23 cm) round cake

For the syrup

1½ cups (360 ml) water

1½ cups (300 g) sugar

¼ cup (70 g) honey

6 whole cloves

2 cinnamon sticks

For the cake

½ cup (120 ml) plus 1 tablespoon vegetable oil

3 large eggs

½ cup (100 g) sugar

1 teaspoon vanilla extract

¼ teaspoon kosher salt

½ cup (120 ml) whole milk

1 cup (125 g) plus 1 heaping tablespoon all-purpose flour

1 teaspoon baking powder

1 teaspoon baking soda

1 heaping teaspoon ground cinnamon

½ teaspoon ground cloves

¼ teaspoon freshly ground nutmeg

1½ cups (150 g) raw walnuts

A classic and simple cake of Greece. This juicy walnut cake is flavored with cinnamon, cloves, and nutmeg and bathed in sweet honey syrup.

Prepare the syrup: In a medium saucepan, mix together the water, the 1½ cups (300 g) sugar, the honey, cloves, and cinnamon sticks. Bring to a boil over medium heat, reduce the heat to low, and simmer uncovered for about 5 minutes, until the sugar and honey dissolve completely and the syrup is clear. Turn off the heat and let cool to room temperature. Remove and discard the cloves and cinnamon sticks.

Prepare the cake: Preheat the oven to 350°F (175°C). Grease a 9-inch (23 cm) springform baking pan with 1 tablespoon of the oil.

In the bowl of a stand mixer fitted with the whisk attachment, beat the eggs, the ½ cup (100 g) sugar, the vanilla, and the salt on medium-high speed for 2 to 3 minutes, until the mixture is light and fluffy. Be careful not to overbeat the eggs. Stop the mixer and add the remaining ½ cup (120 ml) oil and the milk, and mix with a wooden spoon until combined.

In a separate medium bowl, mix together the 1 cup (125 g) flour, the baking powder, baking soda, ground cinnamon, cloves, and nutmeg. Add the flour mixture to the egg mixture, and mix with a wooden spoon until the batter is smooth and uniform.

Put the walnuts in the bowl of a food processor and pulse to coarsely grind them. Remove the blade of the food processor, add the remaining 1 heaping tablespoon flour to the bowl, and mix with a spoon. Add the walnuts to the cake batter and gently fold them in.

Pour the batter into the prepared pan and smooth the surface.

Bake for 25 to 35 minutes, until the cake is golden and a toothpick inserted in the center comes out clean but slightly damp.

Remove the cake from the oven and immediately poke the top of the cake 8 to 12 times with a toothpick or a wooden skewer. Pour

the reserved syrup evenly over the top of the cake. Let cool to room temperature in the pan while the cake absorbs the syrup. Serve in the pan or slice into individual pieces.

Karidopita can be stored covered at room temperature for up to 3 days.

Phyllo Pastry Filled with Walnuts and Pistachios

BAKLAVA

Makes one 9-by-13-inch (23 by 33 cm) pastry

For the syrup

1½ cups (360 ml) water

1½ cups (300 g) sugar

3 tablespoons lemon juice

For the pastry

3 cups (300 g) raw walnuts

1½ cups (195 g) raw shelled pistachios

½ cup (100 g) sugar

1 heaping tablespoon ground cinnamon

½ teaspoon kosher salt

⅔ cup (150 g) butter, melted

14 sheets phyllo dough, thawed overnight in the refrigerator, if frozen

Baklava is an emblematic Greek pastry made from layers of crispy golden phyllo filled with a sugary-spiced walnut mixture, soaked in fragrant sweet syrup. Each person's version is unique, much like a fingerprint. Recipes vary in the number of phyllo sheets in each layer, the amount and contents of the filling, and, of course, the flavoring of the syrup. My variation offers equal layers of the phyllo dough and the walnut and pistachio stuffing, creating a balance of sweetness and texture. Instead of brushing each phyllo sheet with butter separately, which is the traditional method, I pour the melted butter over the cut baklava before baking, which is a nice shortcut.

Prepare the syrup: In a medium saucepan, mix together the water, the 1½ cups (300 g) sugar, and the lemon juice. Bring to a boil over medium heat, reduce the heat to low, and simmer uncovered for about 5 minutes, until the sugar dissolves completely and the syrup is clear. Let it cool to room temperature. Set aside.

Prepare the baklava: Put the walnuts in the bowl of a food processor and pulse to coarsely grind them. Transfer the chopped walnuts to a large bowl.

Put the pistachios in the bowl of the food processor and pulse to coarsely grind them. Transfer the chopped pistachios to the bowl with the walnuts.

Add the ½ cup (100 g) sugar, cinnamon, and salt, and mix.

Preheat the oven to 350°F (175°C). Brush a 9-by-13-inch (23 by 33 cm) glass or metal baking pan with a little melted butter.

On a clean work surface, unroll the phyllo sheets and cover them with a slightly damp kitchen towel to prevent them from drying out while you work with them. If the phyllo sheets are larger than the pan, use kitchen scissors to cut the edges so that they fit snugly in the bottom of the pan. Layer 8 phyllo sheets on the bottom of the pan. Spread the walnut and pistachio mixture evenly over the phyllo. Cover with the remaining 6 phyllo sheets.

Use a sharp knife to cut diamond shapes into the baklava: Working right to left, cut 5 horizontal lines, spacing them 1½ inches (4 cm) apart, piercing the knife all the way down to the bottom of the pan, to get 6 horizontal strips. Then make a diagonal cut from the upper left corner of the pan all the way to the lower right corner. Make 3 parallel lines on either side of that diagonal, 1½ inches (4 cm) apart, to get 4 strips on each side. Precutting makes the baklava much easier to serve, as phyllo dough becomes crisp and crumbly after baking. Gently pour the melted butter evenly over the baklava. The butter must be completely melted when you do this step. If the butter has hardened a little, warm it again.

Bake for 40 to 50 minutes, until the baklava is golden brown.

Remove the baklava from the oven and immediately pour the reserved syrup evenly over the top. Let cool to room temperature in the pan, while the cake absorbs the syrup.

Baklava can be stored covered at room temperature for up to 3 days.

Custard Pie

BOUGATSA

Makes one 9-by-13-inch (23 by 33 cm) pastry

1 cup (2 sticks/230 g) unsalted butter, cut into cubes

⅔ cup (110 g) semolina flour

5 cups (1.2 L) whole milk

1 cup (200 g) granulated sugar

2 teaspoons vanilla extract

½ teaspoon kosher salt

4 large eggs

14 sheets phyllo dough, thawed overnight in the refrigerator if frozen

To serve

3 tablespoons powdered sugar

1 teaspoon ground cinnamon

This sweet phyllo pastry is filled with a creamy custard and garnished with powdered sugar and ground cinnamon. Bougatsa is a popular breakfast in Greece, but it can also be enjoyed as a dessert or a snack.

In a medium pot, melt ½ cup (1 stick/115 g) of the butter over medium heat. Add the semolina flour and cook, stirring constantly with a wooden spoon, for 20 to 30 seconds, until the butter and flour are fully incorporated. Add the milk, granulated sugar, vanilla, and salt, whisking constantly, and bring to a boil over medium-high heat. Reduce the heat to medium and cook, whisking constantly, for 2 to 4 minutes, until the mixture thickens to the consistency of porridge. Remove the pot from the heat.

Remove 1 cup (240 ml) of the semolina mixture from the pot and place it in a small bowl. Set aside.

In a medium bowl, whisk the eggs. To temper the eggs, add the reserved 1 cup (240 ml) of the hot semolina mixture to the eggs and stir immediately. Pour the egg mixture into the pot and stir immediately for 50 to 60 seconds, until the custard batter is smooth and uniform. Let cool for 10 minutes.

Preheat the oven to 350°F (175°C).

Melt the remaining ½ cup (1 stick/115 g) butter in a saucepan or in the microwave. Brush a 9-by-13-inch (23 by 33 cm) glass or metal baking dish with a little melted butter.

On a clean work surface, unroll the phyllo sheets and cover them with a slightly damp kitchen towel. If the phyllo sheets are larger than the pan, use kitchen scissors to cut the edges so that they fit snugly in the bottom of the pan. Layer 2 phyllo sheets on the bottom of the prepared pan and brush the top phyllo sheet with melted butter. Layer 2 more phyllo sheets on top and brush with more of the melted butter. Repeat again with 2 more phyllo sheets and brush with more of the melted butter. Cover with 1 more phyllo sheet for

7 layers of buttered phyllo sheets in total. It's not necessary to brush the seventh phyllo with butter.

If the custard has formed a skin on the top, whisk it to assimilate the crust into the mixture. Pour the custard into the pan and spread it evenly over the phyllo with an offset spatula. Cover with 2 phyllo sheets and brush the top phyllo sheet with melted butter. Add 2 more phyllo sheets and brush the top one with more of the melted butter. Then cover with the remaining 3 phyllo sheets, and brush only the top one with melted butter.

Before baking, use a large knife to cut the top layers of the bougatsa into 18 to 24 squares, cutting through the top layers of phyllo just until you reach the filling. Precutting makes it much easier to serve, as phyllo dough becomes crisp and crumbly after baking.

Bake for 35 to 45 minutes, until the bougatsa is golden brown. Let rest for 20 minutes before cutting and serving.

Sprinkle with the powdered sugar and cinnamon and serve warm or at room temperature.

Bougatsa can be stored covered in the refrigerator for up to 3 days. To reheat, warm in the oven at 325°F (160°C) for 10 to 15 minutes.

Greek Doughnuts

LOUKOUMADES

Makes about 24 small doughnuts

For the syrup

1 cup (200 g) sugar

¾ cup (180 ml) water

½ cup (140 g) honey

1 cinnamon stick

For the doughnuts

1½ cups (360 ml) lukewarm water

2 teaspoons (7 g) active dry yeast

2 tablespoons honey

1 tablespoon sugar

1¾ cups (220 g) all-purpose flour

¼ packed cup (35 g) cornstarch

½ teaspoon kosher salt

1 teaspoon vanilla extract

For frying

4 cups (960 ml) vegetable oil

These small fluffy doughnuts come originally from Turkey, where they are called lokma. Although there are several versions, the basic recipe is the same: a yeast dough deep-fried in bite-size nuggets and covered with a flavorful topping, which can include anything from honey to chocolate or caramel sauces to powdered sugar, sesame seeds, or crushed walnuts or pistachios. This recipe finishes the doughnuts with a cinnamon-flavored honey syrup.

Prepare the syrup: In a medium saucepan, mix together the 1 cup (200 g) sugar, water, ½ cup (140 g) honey, and cinnamon stick. Bring to a boil over medium heat, reduce the heat to low, and simmer uncovered for about 5 minutes, until the sugar and honey dissolve completely and the syrup is clear. Remove from the heat and let cool to room temperature. Remove and discard the cinnamon stick.

Prepare the doughnuts: In a medium bowl, mix the lukewarm water, yeast, 2 tablespoons honey, and 1 tablespoon sugar until the yeast, honey, and sugar dissolve completely. Let sit for 10 minutes, until the mixture is bubbly.

In a large bowl, mix the flour, cornstarch, and salt. Add the yeast mixture and vanilla and whisk until the batter is smooth and uniform. Cover the bowl with plastic wrap and let it sit at room temperature for 50 to 60 minutes, until the batter doubles in size.

Cover a medium skillet with the vegetable oil at least 3 inches (8 cm) deep, and bring to a frying temperature over medium-high heat. You can check the temperature of the oil by dipping the handle of a wooden spoon in it. When the oil is ready, it will gently sizzle and bubble up around the handle.

Line a plate with a paper towel.

Working in batches, fill an ice cream scoop halfway with batter and carefully drop it into the oil. Portion out 5 or 6 doughnuts like this, being careful not to overcrowd the pan, and fry for 2 to 3 minutes on each side, until golden, using a slotted spoon to turn them over.

Scoop out the doughnuts and let them drain on the paper towel–lined plate. Repeat with the rest of the doughnut batter, a quarter at a time.

Transfer the hot loukoumades to a serving plate. Pour the reserved syrup over the doughnuts and serve immediately.

Rice Pudding

RIZOGALO

Serves 4 to 6

⅔ cup (120 g) uncooked short-grain rice, preferably arborio or carnaroli

1½ cups (360 ml) lukewarm water

1 cup (240 ml) whole milk

1 cup (240 ml) heavy cream

½ cup (100 g) sugar

1 teaspoon vanilla extract

While variations of rice pudding are popular in many countries, the Greek version, called rizogalo, is based on an ancient dish called kykeon. Originally the pudding was made of barley, honey, and water, but the barley was later replaced with rice, which was first cultivated in Greece at the beginning of the twentieth century. In this recipe, the rice is first cooked in water until it is semi-tender before the other ingredients are added, which shortens its cooking time. I use both heavy cream and milk, for a richer pudding.

Rinse the rice in a fine-mesh sieve under cold water until the water runs clear, and drain.

Transfer the rice to a medium nonstick pot and add the lukewarm water. Bring to a boil over high heat, reduce the heat to low, and simmer covered for 10 to 12 minutes, until the water is absorbed into the rice but the rice is slightly undercooked.

Add the milk, cream, sugar, and vanilla, and mix. Bring to a boil over medium-high heat (watch that the milk and cream don't bubble over), reduce the heat to low, and cook uncovered, stirring occasionally with a wooden spoon, for 15 to 20 minutes, until the rice is very tender and the pudding is thick.

Spoon the rizogalo into small glass bowls or ramekins, and serve warm or cold.

Rizogalo can be stored covered in the refrigerator for up to 4 days.

Honey Sesame Bars

PASTELI

Makes about 12 pasteli

1 tablespoon light olive oil or vegetable oil

1¼ cups (150 g) sesame seeds

½ cup (140 g) honey

¼ teaspoon kosher salt

Pasteli, also known as Greek sesame candy, is a traditional snack in Greece made with sesame seeds and honey, and sometimes with pistachios or other nuts for additional crunch. The beauty of this treat is that a simple version can be made with only four ingredients.

Brush two pieces of parchment paper, at least 13 by 16 inches (33 by 41 cm), with a little oil.

Place the sesame seeds in a large nonstick pan and toast them over medium heat, stirring constantly with a wooden spoon, for 2 to 3 minutes, until golden.

Add the honey and salt and cook, stirring constantly, for 2 to 3 minutes, until the mixture comes together and becomes thick and sticky.

Scoop the sesame mixture onto the greased side of one piece of the parchment paper. Place the other piece of parchment greased-side down on top of the sesame mixture. Use a rolling pin to spread the sesame mixture into a rectangle that is about ¼ inch (6 mm) thick. Let cool to room temperature.

Remove the top parchment paper and cut the sesame candy into 12 bars, 1½ by 2¾ inches (4 by 7 cm) each.

Pasteli can be stored in an airtight container at room temperature for up to 7 days.

Sweet Orange Peel Preserve

GLIKO KOUTALIOU PORTOKALI

Makes 6 cups (1.5 kg)

6 medium oranges, unpeeled, washed and scrubbed well

5 cups (1 kg) sugar

3 cups (720 ml) water

3 tablespoons lemon juice

Preserved fruits or vegetables are traditionally used as a treat for festive celebrations or as a way to welcome guests into one's home. They are often served on a silver tray with glasses of cold water, and you can enjoy preserved orange peels alongside cakes, on toast, as a topping for yogurt or ice cream, or as an addition to cheese boards. This recipe is also a great way to use up orange peels instead of throwing them away after you've enjoyed the fruit. To give the orange preserves their recognizable curly shape, the strips of orange peel are tightly coiled and then threaded onto a piece of kitchen twine. Boiling the peels in water several times before they are candied in a simple syrup takes away the bitter flavor.

Use a paring knife to cut each orange peel vertically from top to bottom into 8 strips. Cut a 24-inch (60 cm) length of kitchen twine. Pass the twine through the eye of a large needle and tie a knot at the end. Tightly coil a strip of orange peel and thread it onto the string with the needle. Alternatively, you can use toothpicks, one per peel. Continue threading the peels from 2 oranges until you have a chain of 16 coiled peels. Remove the needle and tie off the end with another knot. Repeat with the rest of the orange peels to get 3 chains in total.

Place the orange peel chains in a large pot and cover with room-temperature water. Bring to a boil over high heat and then drain the water. Once again, cover the orange peels with water, bring to a boil over high heat, and drain the water. Repeat this process four more times, for a total of six times.

In a large saucepan, mix the sugar, water, and lemon juice. Bring to a boil over medium heat, reduce the heat to low, and simmer uncovered for about 5 minutes, until the sugar dissolves completely and the syrup is clear.

Add the orange peel chains to the syrup in one layer and cook uncovered over medium-low heat for 40 to 50 minutes, until the peels become translucent and the syrup thickens. Use a slotted

spoon to skim off the foam throughout the cooking. Let cool to room temperature.

Cut the ends of the strings and pull off the candied orange peels. Discard the strings.

Transfer the orange peels and the syrup to a clean jar and seal.

Gliko koutaliou portokali can be stored in the refrigerator for up to 6 months. Use a clean spoon to remove orange peels from the jar.

Cherry Spoon Preserve

GLIKO KOUTALIOU KERASI

Makes 4 cups (1 kg)

2 pounds (900 g) cherries
½ cup (120 ml) water
3 tablespoons lemon juice
1 teaspoon vanilla extract
4½ cups (900 g) sugar

Spoon sweets, preserved fruits served in a spoon as a gesture of hospitality, are popular throughout Greece, and cherry spoon preserve is one of the best versions. This is a foolproof recipe; it always comes out, no matter what type of cherry is used.

Rinse the cherries in a colander under cold water, and drain. Remove the stems and use a cherry pitter to remove the pits. While you work, place the pitted cherries in a large pot and collect the pits and any juices released from the cherries in a separate bowl. (You may want to wear disposable plastic or latex kitchen gloves to prevent your hands from staining when you do this.) Pour the ½ cup (120 ml) water into the small bowl with the pits and stir. (This will help extract a little more flavor from the pits.)

Use a fine-mesh sieve to strain the liquid from the pits and add the liquid to the pot with cherries. Add the lemon juice and vanilla and mix.

Sprinkle the sugar evenly over the cherries, cover the pot with plastic wrap, and transfer to the refrigerator overnight.

Put a small plate in the freezer. This will be used to check whether the preserves are ready.

The next day, heat the pot over medium-high heat. Do not stir, just shake the pot until the sugar dissolves. (Be careful that the liquid doesn't bubble over.) Reduce the heat to medium and cook uncovered, stirring occasionally, for 45 to 55 minutes, until the liquid has the consistency of maple syrup. Use a slotted spoon to skim off the foam throughout the cooking.

To check if the cherries are ready, remove your frozen plate from the freezer and place a teaspoon of the syrup on the plate. Run your finger through it. If the path remains, the preserves are ready. If not, cook it for a few more minutes. Let cool to room temperature.

Transfer the cherry preserves to a clean jar and seal.

Gliko koutaliou kerasi can be stored in the refrigerator for up to 6 months. Use a clean spoon to remove cherry preserves from the jar.

Quinces Baked in Red Wine

KIDONIA PSITA

Serves 6 to 8

4 medium quinces, skin on, washed and scrubbed well

2 cups (480 ml) dry red wine

2 cups (400 g) sugar

1 cup (240 ml) water

2 tablespoons lemon juice

6 whole cloves

3 cinnamon sticks

To serve:

Full-fat Greek yogurt or whipped cream

Quinces are a versatile fruit that can be used in both savory and sweet dishes. When raw, quinces are very hard and bitter, but when cooked or baked, they become soft and sweet. This dessert is perfect for the chilly fall, when quinces are in season. The wine and warm spices give the quinces depth and great flavor, and after a day or two, they are even tastier.

Preheat the oven to 350°F (175°C).

Using a large sharp knife, cut the quinces into quarters and remove the cores. Place the quinces in a 9-by-13-inch (23 by 33 cm) glass or ceramic baking dish, cut-side down.

In a medium saucepan, mix together the wine, sugar, water, lemon juice, cloves, and cinnamon sticks. Bring to a boil over medium heat, reduce the heat to low, and simmer uncovered for about 5 minutes, until the sugar dissolves. Gently pour the wine mixture over the quinces and cover the pan with aluminum foil.

Bake for 70 minutes. Remove the pan from the oven and take off the aluminum foil. Use tongs to turn the quinces over so that the cut side is now up.

Return the pan to the oven and bake uncovered for 30 to 35 minutes, until the quinces are tender and golden.

Remove the pan from the oven. Use tongs to turn the quinces over once more, so that the cut side is down again. Let cool in the syrup to room temperature.

Serve the baked quinces at room temperature or cold with thick yogurt.

Kidonia psita can be stored in an airtight container in the refrigerator for up to 3 days.

QUINCES

In ancient Greece, quinces were often used in stews, pies, and jams. They were also used as the base for kydonium, an alcoholic drink made from fermented quinces, honey, and spices that was served at weddings and other special occasions.

From reading Greek mythology, many people may be familiar with the symbol of the golden apple as the precipitating cause of the Trojan War. However, what is less well-known is that the golden apple might in fact have been a quince. As the story goes, Hera, Athena, and Aphrodite all laid claim to the golden apple, whose inscription τῇ καλλίστῃ (tē kallistē), meaning "to the fairest," declared its owner to be the most beautiful of the goddesses. In an effort to bribe the Trojan prince Paris into declaring her the rightful owner of the apple, each goddess offered him a different prize. In the end, Paris accepted Aphrodite's bribe of the most beautiful woman in the world, for which he received Helen of Troy, wife of Menelaus, the king of Sparta. The abduction of Helen led to the Trojan War, which lasted ten years and ended with the destruction of Troy.

For those who believe that the golden apple was in fact a quince, the fruit has become a symbol of beauty, power, destruction, and even fertility and childbirth.

THE HONEY OF GREECE

At midnight on Christmas Eve, in the villages of central Greece, the unmarried women anoint the communal water faucets with honey and butter. In this custom, known as the feeding of the fountain, these women must walk to the nearest public water fountain, in olden times the only source of drinkable water for the entire village, to bring back the "speechless water" (speechless because nobody speaks a word as they make their way to the fountain). It is said that the girl who gets to the water fountain first will be the luckiest all year. After the water is collected, they lather the tap attached to the fountain with butter and honey, with the wish that as the water runs, so will the water flow in the house, and as sweet as honey is, so sweet will be life. Once everyone returns home, all of the family members have a drink from the water that was collected, and the rest of the water is sprinkled around the house to spread its sweet luck.

Honey has always played an important part in Greece's history and cultural life. According to myth, baby Zeus was sustained on the honey of sacred bees, and when he became king of the gods, honey was enthroned as a food of the gods. Ancient Greeks believed that bees could foretell the weather and had prophetic powers. It was said that the buzz of foraging wild bees heralded the arrival of spring each year. Artemis, Apollo's twin sister and the goddess of forests, animals, and fertility, is associated with bees; the ancient Greeks made libations with wine and honey and baked small honey buns in her honor.

Clay pots used for smoking wild bees and for storing beeswax dated to the sixth millennium BCE demonstrate that people in Greece have been using bee products since at least the Neolithic period. Aristaeus, Apollo's son, is said to have passed the knowledge of beekeeping first to the people of the island of Kea, but the systematic cultivation of beehives began in the island of Crete during the second millennium BCE, and from there the practice spread to the rest of the ancient Greek world. One of the earliest beehives in Greece can be found on the island of Santorini, where it survived the volcanic explosion that vaporized most of the island in the early 1600s BCE.

In antiquity, honey was used in cooking, medicine, ceremonies, and more. The honey of Athens was famous for its high quality, and the city became rich exporting it around the Mediterranean. Athenian food markets were full of honey-based treats, including tiganitae, wheat pancakes covered in honey, and milomela, apples preserved in honey, a predecessor of the modern-day candied apple. Hippocrates, the father of Western medicine, advised everyone, especially the sick and old, to eat honey, as he believed it strengthened the human body. Pythagoras and his followers are said to have eaten a diet almost exclusively based on honey, and Democritus, a Greek philosopher known for theorizing about the atom, attributed his own considerable longevity to a heavy consumption of honey wine. Honey was also used as a medicine for fevers, an ointment for wounds and rashes, a cough reliever, and a mouthwash,

for converts from the ancient Greek religions, who did not use candles in their rituals. Orthodox iconography proliferated after the technique of creating paintings from hot beeswax colored with pigments was discovered.

Bees thrive in modern-day Greece because the country is rich with a variety of wild flora to feed on. Throughout the year, Greek beekeepers move their hives near whatever plants are in bloom, a practice followed since antiquity. The honey they collect is gathered at the end of each feeding cycle and is classified based on the plant the bees fed on during that season. Honey harvested in spring is defined by the flowers that blossom at that time. Honey collected in summer is flavored with thyme, while late-summer honey is redolent of pine and fall honey tastes like chestnuts. Flower honey is usually the sweetest, but thyme honey, which is unique to Greece, is considered the most aromatic. Pine honey is the most mineral-rich. Today Greece is one of the top honey producers in the European Union. The honey from Attica continues to be famed for its quality, but it is the island of Crete, which introduced the cultivation of bees to the rest of Greece, that boasts the highest population of bees per capita in the world.

and even as a cosmetic. The power of honey was indisputable. In fact, Alexander the Great's body is said to have been placed in a sarcophagus filled with honey so it could be preserved for eternity.

With the advent of Christianity, honey and beekeeping became even more important. In Greek Orthodoxy, honey symbolizes the sweetness of the divine message of eternal life. Beeswax was used to produce the candles used in religious settings, a new practice

Acknowledgments

Yassou is a dream come true, and it could not have happened without the help of many dear people who made it a reality. Thank you to my publisher, Lia Ronnen, for believing in this cookbook and giving me the opportunity—I am forever grateful. To the entire Artisan team, especially Bella Lemos, Judy Pray, Laura Cherkas, and Suet Chong, for your professionalism, kindness, and uncompromising thoroughness. To Amit Farber, for your beautiful and accurate styling that brought the spirit of Greece to these pages, and for your friendship, encouragement, and investment of countless hours beyond the days of photography. To Amir Menahem, for your mouthwatering photographs, hard work and devotion, always with a smile, and a perfect Greek palate for tasting all the recipes in this book. To Leonidas Vournelis, for your excellent writing, wisdom, and relentless knowledge. To Margarita Manousou, for guiding us through the streets of Greece during the atmospheric shots. To Yannis Evangelou, for taking us on a moving and educational trip on Kea. To Géraldine Ganne, for graciously opening your boutique hive and gorgeous house on Kea to us. To Ophir Harel, for allowing us to photograph the creation of olive oil in your amazing olive press. To Annabelle Balilahon, for your invaluable assistance in the kitchen, washing, cleaning, cutting, chopping, grating, and measuring ingredients. I could not have done it without you on set.

To my friends Adeena Sussman, Iris Shimonov, Tal Shaked, Shira Klein, Mali Shivek, Yael Oren, Guy Yamen, Israel Varsano, Michal Yanai, and Juliana Nahmias, for your wise advice and support. To all the gifted cooks who shared the secrets of Greek cuisine with me ever since my childhood and taught me how to cook: my late grandmother Levana Angel; my mother, Miri Angel; my aunt Sarah Angel; my late aunt Rebecca Bachar; and my uncle Itzik Angel. To my late father, Joseph Angel, who instilled in me the love of Greek food and music that flows through my veins. **To the people of Greece: your passion for life, contagious cheerfulness, generous hospitality, and love of simple and authentic food truly inspire me.** To the loves of my life: my husband, Rafi, and children, Itamar and Abigail. You three are my engine, my anchor, and my happiness. I love you more than words can say.

Index

Page numbers in *italics* refer to photos.

SHAILY LIPA was born and raised in Tel Aviv to a family of Greek and Turkish origin. She is a culinary and lifestyle expert and TV personality. She invites her audience to take part in her cooking and hosting adventures at home via her Instagram account, @shailylipa. Lipa has written eleven best-selling cookbooks in Israel. This is her first English-language cookbook.